Frivolous Lawsuits and Frivolous Defenses

Recent Titles from Quorum Books

The Right of Privacy in the Computer Age
Warren Freedman

Information and Records Management: A Decision-Maker's Guide to Systems Planning and Implementation
Milburn D. Smith III

Marketing and the Quality-of-Life Interface
A. Coskun Samli, editor

Energy Resources Development: Politics and Policies
Richard L. Ender and John Choon Kim, editors

International Law of Take-Overs and Mergers: Southern Europe, Africa, and the Middle East
H. Leigh Ffrench

Law, Policy, and Optimizing Analysis
Stuart S. Nagel

Six Roundtable Discussions of Corporate Finance with Joel Stern
Donald H. Chew, Jr., editor

Trading Energy Futures: A Manual for Energy Industry Professionals
Stewart L. Brown and Steven Errera

Selecting and Installing Software Packages: New Methodology for Corporate Implementation
Jud Breslin

Creative Problem Solving: A Guide for Trainers and Management
Arthur B. VanGundy

The Business Systems Development Process: A Management Perspective
Roger E. Walters

Quantitative Models in Accounting: A Procedural Guide for Professionals
Ahmed Belkaoui

Frivolous Lawsuits and Frivolous Defenses

Unjustifiable Litigation

Warren Freedman

Q Quorum Books
NEW YORK • WESTPORT, CONNECTICUT • LONDON

Library of Congress Cataloging-in-Publication Data

Freedman, Warren.
Frivolous lawsuits and frivolous defenses.

Bibliography: p.
Includes index.
1. Frivolous suits (Civil procedure)—United States.
I. Title.
KF8887.F74 1987 347.73′5 86-20522
347.3075
ISBN 0-89930-188-6 (lib. bdg. : alk. paper)

Library of Congress Catalog Card Number: 86-20522
ISBN: 0-89930-188-6

First published in 1987 by Quorum Books

Greenwood Press, Inc.
88 Post Road West, Westport, Connecticut 06881

Printed in the United States of America

The paper used in this book complies with the Permanent Paper Standard issued by the National Information Standards Organization (Z39.48-1984).

10 9 8 7 6 5 4 3 2 1

Contents

Frivolous Lawsuits and Frivolous Defenses

1

Frivolity and Unjustifiable Litigation

1.1 THE FRIVOLOUS CLAIM

The term "frivolous" has been legally defined as "given to triflings, not worth notice" and "of little weight or importance, not worth notice or slight" (37 CJS, 1382). As an adjective modifying the noun "claim," the clear meaning is that the claim is without arguable merit both in law and in fact (Hogan v. Midland County Commissioners Court, 680 F2d, 1101, 5th Cir, 1982). In Tomasello v. Trump (217 NYS2d 304, 1961) the New York Supreme Court, Queens County, in a derivative stockholders' action for waste and to compel the declaration of dividends, defined the term "frivolous" as connoting "an objection so clearly and palpably without merit as to indicate bad faith on the part of the party making it without the necessity of even argument to convince the court there-of." And in Sims v. Zolango (481 F Supp 388, SDNY, 1979) the federal district court in New York looked into the per se action by a prisoner against the warden, doctor, and various staff members of the jail. Here the prisoner alleged violation of his civil rights by defendants' unwarranted force and by subjecting him to mental torture. The court observed that the prisoner had been handcuffed to cell bars or mattress, that the prisoner had lit fires in his cell, that the prisoner had slashed his wrists, and that the prisoner had struck prison guards. Nevertheless, the action was deemed "frivolous" under 28 USC 1915(d) as one in which the plaintiff's realistic chances of success are slight:

> When Sims' present allegations are examined against the background of his earlier lawsuits and his most recent submissions, I conclude that this action is frivolous and should

be dismissed pursuant to 28 USC Section 1915 (d). I am completely satisfied that the allegations of official misconduct which purport to state a claim under Section 1983 are without merit. Sims may well have been handcuffed to the cell bars or the mattress or may have been struck by a prison officer, but Sims' own statement of the facts set forth the justification for such conduct. Sims admits that he lights fires; he admits that he has slashed his wrists on more than one occasion to attract attention; and he admits that he first struck a prison guard before he was subdued by other guards. Under the foregoing circumstances, stripped of its hyperbole, the instant complaint merely documents the necessary and understandable reaction of prison officials to the dangerous behavior of a disturbed prisoner.

In the context of prison life, as well as the life of an indigent, it is well to note Clark v. Zimmerman (394 F Supp 1166, MD Pa, 1975), where that court observed:

Persons proceeding in forma pauperis are immune from imposition of costs if they are unsuccessful; and because of their poverty, they are practically immune from later tort actions for ''malicious prosecution'' or abuse of process. Thus indigents, unlike other litigants, approach the courts in a context where they have nothing to lose and everything to gain. The temptation to file complaints that contain facts which cannot be proved is obviously stronger in such a situation. For convicted prisoners with much idle time and free paper, ink, law books, and mailing privileges the temptation is especially strong.

Indeed, federal district courts are readily given the authority to dismiss ''frivolous'' actions brought in *forma pauperis*.

Another frivolous claim was presented in Daniell v. Ford Motor Co. (581 F Supp 84, NM, 1983), where the plaintiff admitted that she was depressed, and, in an attempt to commit suicide, she locked herself in the trunk of her 1973 Ford automobile, where she remained for nine days. She then sued Ford Motor Company for her physical and psychological injuries arising from that occurrence. She contended that the automobile had a design defect because the trunk lock did not have an internal release mechanism which would have permitted her to escape, assuming that she was sufficiently sane to want to escape. Furthermore, Ford Motor Company had not warned her of the dangerous condition if she stowed away in her own automobile trunk! Although the court dismissed the claim as ''frivolous,'' the court felt impelled to provide an elaborate delineation of such issues as foreseeability of harm, intended purposes of an automobile trunk, and Ford's duty to warn of known dangers.

As a general rule, if an argument is required to show that the pleading is bad or frivolous, then the pleading is not frivolous (Maccarone v. Hayes, 82 NYS 1005, 1903). A frivolous pleading is one interposed for delay and indicates by its character its bad faith (Lerdall v. Charter Oak Life Insurance Co., 8 NW 280, Wis, 1981). The pleading must be so palpably false on its face that mere inspection indicates the bad faith of the plaintiff in his pleading (Etiwan Fertilizer Co. v. Johns, 24 SE2d 74, SC, 1930). The frivolous pleading is clearly and incontrovertibly void of significance or futile in point of law as to indicate bad faith (Mann v. Luke, 68 NYS2d 313, 1947). But where counsel for the defense found it necessary to submit a reply brief of 7,000 words, the pleading was deemed not to be frivolous (Lloyd v. Ballantine, 45 NYS 809, 1897). A pleading is frivolous where there is clearly no defense that can be set up nor is any defense expected (Hill v. Warner, 57 NYS 355, 1899).

A "sham pleading" is defined as one good on its face but false in fact, and is readily distinguishable from a frivolous pleading, which is insufficient on its face, although possibly true in fact (Holdman v. Tansey, 151 A 874, NJ, 1930). Both pleadings, however, are within the judicial prerogative to strike out (Rhea v. Hacknew, 157 So 190, Fla, 1934). In Bittner v. Sadoff & Rudoy Industries (728 F2d 820, 6th Cir, 1984) the court dismissed the suit for attorney's fees when it found that the suit was so completely without hope of succeeding that it inferred that plaintiff brought it to harass defendant rather than to obtain a favorable judgment. In Malone v. Colyer (710 F2d 258, 7th Cir, 1983) it appeared beyond doubt that plaintiff could prove no set of facts which would entitle him to relief. Where the allegations against the Illinois Pollution Control Board were, for the most part, void of facts reasonably informing defendants of the manner and the extent to which the Environmental Protection Act and/or regulations were being violated, the Illinois court held the pleading to be frivolous or "duplicitous" and affirmed the failure to hold a hearing (Rocke v. Illinois Pollution Control Board, 297 NE2d 51, 1978).

In Ware v. State of New York, the New York Court of Claims incredibly asserted that "plaintiff must only demonstrate that her position is not frivolous, and further information may establish her cause of action." The decision, dated January 6, 1986, continued the motion to dismiss by the defendant state which was sued by a mother on behalf of her three-year-old daughter who was sexually assaulted in May 1984 at a state-operated day care center. The plaintiff mother was unable to file her claim for thirteen months after the sexual assault until June 1985 because the state of New York did not deliver the requested day care center records to the plaintiff until October 1985. In August 1985 the defendant state of New York had moved to dismiss for failure to state a cause of action; the state contended that various acts or omissions were of a "discretionary" character and therefore the state was not liable. The court agreed that further discovery was needed, continued the motion to dismiss, but said nothing derogatory about the state for its failure to comply with discovery requests. Plaintiff mother's suit simply cannot be termed "frivolous," as the court intimated.

The problem with the "frivolous claim" is simply that there are too many of them. It is like a disease that is pervasive as well as malignant. Professor Dan Hurley in his "Much Ado About Nothing: An Epidemic of Frivolous Law

Suits Is Turning Our Legal System into the Courtroom of the Absurd'' (17 Docket Call 14-17, 1982) sets forth the following cases as examples that have plagued the judicial system:

—a grocer's suit against a patron for eating a grape in his supermarket without paying for it;

—a patient's suit against his dentist for $85.63 in compensation after being forced to wait one hour forty-seven minutes for his appointment;

—an attorney's suit against Jimmy the Groundhog for mistakenly forecasting an early spring;

—a fan's suit against the Chicago Bears for misrepresenting itself as a professional football team;

—a $10 million federal class action suit against professional baseball on behalf of all fans allegedly injured by the 1982 baseball strike;

—a suitor's action against a young woman for the price of flowers and a theatre ticket after she cancelled her promise to date him;

—a suitor's claim for worker's compensation benefits for ''industrial injury to his nervous system'' after the suitor quit work when a co-worker refused to date him;

—an inmate's nuisance suit on the grounds that a newly installed toilet seat was too cold;

—another inmate's nuisance suit that he had lost friends because his brand of deodorant was no longer carried by the prison commissary.

While the above listing of cases is humorous, it should be observed that the court action or the claim itself may be vexatious, in bad faith, dilatory, harassing, abusive, redundant, a sham, or simply irrelevant behavior. A frivolous lawsuit or a frivolous claim embraces all these modes of behavior and others, and the challenge for the legal system is to eliminate these claims and not unfairly discourage claims of potential substance without jeopardizing the very operation of the legal system. A fabulous example of time-consuming and almost wasteful litigation is Nemeroff v. Abelson (469 F Supp 630, SDNY, 1979), where the federal district court wrote a twelve-page opinion in order to conclude that the complaint was frivolous and filed in bad faith; on appeal, the Second U.S. Court of Appeals (620 F2d 339, 1980) reversed in an equally long opinion, after reviewing ten main and reply briefs and an appendix of over 1,200 pages, and held that the original complaint had merit and was not frivolous nor had it been filed in bad faith. After all, when two courts consumed so much time and effort in considering the matter, it would appear that the claim simply could not have been frivolous in the first instance!

American industry has been particularly aroused by the great volume of litigation, as has the Chief Justice of the United States, who in 1985 lamented that our society today ''has an almost irrational focus—virtually a mania—on litigation as the way to solve all problems.'' Robert H. Malott, chairman of the board and chief executive officer of FMC Corporation, delivered an address at the Northwestern University Law School Corporate Counsel Institute on October 10, 1985, "America's Liability Explosion: Can We Afford the Cost?" in which he cited three cases of litigation which "strain credulity," to wit:

> *Item*: Two Maryland men decided to dry their hot air balloon in a commercial laundry dryer. The dryer exploded, injuring them. They sued the manufacturer of the dryer and ended up winning nearly $900,000 in damages.
>
> *Item*: An overweight man with a history of coronary disease suffered a heart attack while trying to start a Sears lawnmower. He sued Sears, charging that too much force was required to yank the mower's pull rope. A jury in Pennsylvania awarded him one million dollars, plus another $500,000 in pre-judgment interest.
>
> *Item*: A two-year-old child being treated in the hospital for bronchial spasms suffered brain damage from a drug overdose. Although the hospital staff had clearly exceeded the dosage level prescribed by both the attending doctor and the drug manufacturer, the child's parents successfully sued the company producing the drug. The jury award: nine million dollars in compensation and $13 million in punitive damages.

Malott then continued: "If you think these are isolated cases of absurdly generous liability awards, you are wrong. Last year, awards of a million dollars or more were given in more than 360 personal injury suits—an incredible 13 times the number 10 years ago." Implicit in Malott's remarks is the increasing prominence of frivolous claims in the United States compared with Europe and Japan, which "rarely use the legal system to resolve disputes and, in fact, tend to consider litigation as a form of harassment." Malott concluded that in the United States "this litigation mentality cannot continue. . . . The challenge before us is to arrest the dangerous trend toward excessive litigation."

The frivolous claim is simply not curbed by such legal, scholarly pronouncements as the Restatement (Second) of Torts, which in Comment d to Section 674 states that an attorney who initiates a civil proceeding on behalf of his client or one who takes any steps in the proceeding is not liable if he has probable cause for his action (as defined in Section 675); and, even if he has no probable cause and is convinced that this client's claim is unfounded, he is still not liable if he acts primarily for the purpose of aiding his client in obtaining a proper adjudication of his claim, as under Section 676. The simple fact is that the Restatement opines that an attorney is neither required nor expected to prejudge his client's claim for its frivolity, and although he is fully aware that the claim's chances of success are comparatively slight, it is his responsibility to present the claim to the court for proper adjudication if his client so insists after the attorney has explained to the client the possibilities of success and failure.

1.2 THE FRIVOLOUS ANSWER

The answer filed or served by the defendant is said to be frivolous when it is so clearly bad as to require no argument to show its character and when it is so manifestly defective as to be indicative of bad faith upon mere inspection (Gruenstein v. Biersack, 37 NYS 538, 1896). The answer is frivolous when it does not controvert the material allegations of the preceding complaint and is presumably interposed for mere purposes of delay or to embarrass the plaintiff (Colboch v. Aviation Credit Corp., 166 P2d 584, Ariz. 1946). An answer which is but a repetition of a former answer that was adjudged insufficient is frivolous (State ex rel Kiesel's Estate v. Bishop, 129 P2d 276, Ore, 1942).

A frivolous answer can be manifestly impertinent, as alleging matters which, whether true or false, do not affect the plaintiff's right to recover (Erwin v. Lowery, 64 NC 321, 1980). In Zaveloff v. Zaveloff (37 NYS2d 46, 1942) the action was to partition realty and for an accounting; although the parties' common ownership was a matter of public record, the defendant's answer consisted of denials based on lack of knowledge or information sufficient to form a belief of common ownership. The New York court found the answer to be "frivolous" and a "sham" within rules authorizing treating as a nullity sham or frivolous answers, and the court rendered judgment for the plaintiff accordingly. Similarly, where the answer denies no material averment in the complaint, the answer is deemed not to constitute a defense and is frivolous. But where it cannot be said of an answer that it controverts no material allegation in the complaint, or that the answer is manifestly insufficient, or that it fails to deny the allegations of the complaint, it cannot be said to be frivolous; to make an answer frivolous, the objection must extend to and embrace the whole answer, so that nothing is left of it (Peacock, Hunt & West Co. v. Williams, 110 F 915, 1901).

A defense containing merely evidential matter can be stricken out as "frivolous" (Hespe v. Corning Glass Works, 9 F Supp 725, DCNY). A "frivolous demurrer" is one which raises no serious question of law (Morgan v. Harris, 54 SE 381, NC, 1906).

1.3 THE FRIVOLOUS APPEAL

The definition of a frivolous appeal is a basic question that confronts the appellate court which must look at the case itself to ascertain whether it is without merit and has little chance to succeed, and then the court must look at the conduct of the appellant to see whether he is dilatory, seeks to harass the court or the adversary, or simply desires to mislead the court. The merits of an appeal should be less difficult to spot than a frivolous complaint, for the appeal is a claim that already has undergone judicial scrutiny. Professor Hermann in his article "Frivolous Criminal Appeals" (47 *N.Y.S. Law Review* 701, 1972), however, assessed the criminal appeal in these terms:

> It is an appeal with all or most of the following attributes. It is a loser, not just a probable loser, but a clearly hopeless loser, in the judgment of counsel who have read the record and researched the law. The record contains few, if any, motions or objections by defense counsel. No novel matter of constitutional law or statutory interpretation was raised below or is presented by the facts. The evidence of guilt is so overwhelming that most errors, even if clearly shown to be such, would have to be regarded as harmless ones. There is no evidence on or outside the record of official misconduct or overreaching tactics by the police or prosecution. Nothing which might strike a sympathetic chord in a reasonable person, either with regard to the defendant's character or his involvement in the crime, is presented by the facts of the case. The only matters even tenuously assignable as error are evidentiary rulings which pertain to matters of small consequence, were not objected to in the trial court and can be faulted only by an abstruse exegesis of the law.

Such sardonic wisdom is not particularly enlightening, nor is the U.S. Supreme Court opinion in Anders v. California (386 US 738, 1967), where a court-appointed attorney sought permission to withdraw from representing a criminal client on appeal as the attorney believed the appeal was frivolous. The court ruled that the right to effective assistance of counsel on appeal means the right to have one's lawyer place before the reviewing or appellate court all the points of law and of fact which might arguably support a reversal of conviction. It is not counsel's task to decide that the appeal is frivolous. But if the attorney still wants to withdraw for the same reason of frivolity, he must file "a brief referring to anything on the record that might arguably support the appeal." This schizophrenic opinion of the highest court is perhaps typical of the very problem that confronts both bench and bar in ascertaining when and if a particular appeal is frivolous. Willful delay, refusal to attend depositions, failure to appear at court hearings, and similar instances of improper conduct by an attorney evidence bad faith that would stigmatize a subsequent appeal as frivolous. Misleading the court, such as misquoting a case by leaving out a sentence that undercuts the appellant's position, would also be grounds for deciding that the appeal is frivolous (McCandless v. Great Atlantic & Pacific Tea Co., 697 F2d 198, 7th Cir, 1983).

In the final analysis, where no justiciable question is presented, the appeal is recognized as devoid of merit in that there is little prospect that it can ever succeed, and it is therefore "frivolous" (Collis v. Zoning Hearing Board, 465 A2d 53, Pa, 1983). Damages are available for a "frivolous appeal," as where it manifestly appears that the appeal was taken solely for the purpose of delay and that appealing counsel does not seriously believe in the position he advocates (Bellard v. Safeway Insurance Co., 442 So2d 1313, La App, 1983). An appeal is "frivolous" where it presents no debatable question or no reasonable possibility of reversal (U.S. v. Martone, 283 F Supp 77, P.R., 1968). Other factors supporting a finding of "frivolous appeal" are the lack of credibility of the allegations, the motive for harassment, and court records exposing previous similar claims (Green v. Wilson, 517 F Supp 332, Ky, 1981). Where the brief on appeal clearly misstated the evidence and where there was apparent failure to research the law and supply authority for the point appealed, the Missouri appellate court held the appeal to be "frivolous," warranting an award of $1,000 damages (Jensen v. Jensen, 670 SW2d 16, Mo App, 1984). Double costs of an appeal were awarded in Mead v. Rudnick (35 NE2d 485, Mass, 1941) because the appellant's appeal from an order denying a new trial was based only on the argument that the verdict was against the weight of evidence and that the damages were excessive. Where the appeal was totally lacking in merit, framed with no relevant supporting law, conclusory in nature, and utterly unsupported by any evidence, the Second U.S. Court of Appeals slapped the appellant with double costs and $500 in attorney's fees in favor of the federal government in U.S. v. Potamkin Cadillac Corp. (689 F2d, 2nd Cir, 1982).

Where a defendant made no appearance in an action brought against him on a promissory note, was not presented by counsel, and where the record of the default was duly sustained as the basis for judgment, the appeal was "frivolous" and a 5 percent penalty was imposed on the judgment in Columbia Finance, Inc., v. Romaguera (40 So2d 749, La App, 1949).

Levying fines upon litigants bringing frivolous appeals was encouraged by the U.S. Supreme Court in Hyde v. Van Wormer, decided in late November 1985. Here the court fined the plaintiff, who filed the case pro se the sum of $1,000; plaintiff was attempting to argue that paper currency is not legal tender, and that the writers of the U.S. Constitution intended the dollar to be fixed in value and pegged to the worth of Spanish gold coins! The three dissenters argued that the highest court's rule "set no standards for determining when a petition for certiorari is 'frivolous' . . . [therefore] any award of damages imposed by the court can only be arbitrary."

In the California case of Song v. Smatko (208 Cal Rptr 300, 1984) there was a jury award to a restaurant owner based upon the defendant-doctor's failure to diagnose in a timely manner the patient's breast cancer until the breast cancer had irreversibly spread or metastasized to other parts of her body. The defendant's motion for a new trial was denied, and the doctor and his insurance carrier filed an appeal which the California appellate court described in these terms:

> We find that his appeal and the persistence in prosecuting it demonstrates that it was taken for improper motives—to harass the plaintiff, delay the effect of the judgment to the defendant's financial advantage, and as a bludgeon in an effort to obtain a discounted settlement. . . . We have catalogued the many delaying tactics taken by the defendant on this purported appeal. . . . Defendant's motives in this case are as easy to understand as they are difficult to hide.

The facts revealed that the defendant had strung out the appeal for 2¼ years as the uncompensated plaintiff was dying: "Given the plaintiff's now almost nonexistent life expectancy, defendant's conduct is unconscionable." The court declared that the defendant physician demonstrated "a shocking ignorance of and conscious disregard for the statutes and rules governing post-judgment remedies."

One of the landmark cases on whether or not an appeal is frivolous is In Re Marriage of Flaherty (646 P2d 179, Cal, 1982), wherein an interlocutory judgment dissolving the marriage incorporated prior orders awarding child custody to the husband with visitation rights to the wife and with no child support payable by the wife to the husband. The husband appealed the denial of child support as well as the division of transportation costs for the visitations. The California Court of Appeals affirmed, and fined the husband's attorney $500 for filing the frivolous appeal; but the California Supreme Court reversed, finding that the husband's appeal was not frivolous:

> [A]n appeal should be held to be frivolous only when it is prosecuted for an improper motive—to harass the respondent or delay the effect of an adverse judgment—or when it indisputably has no merit—when any reasonable attorney would agree that the appeal is totally and completely without merit.

The California Supreme Court opined that the appeal actually raised substantial questions of family law in a changing society: "It was not unreasonable for the husband's counsel to think the issues were arguable. There are at least two sides to every legal dispute, and reasonable attorneys will often disagree about the merits of a particular case." The standard imposed by the court was subjective, although the objective standard of lack of good faith was clearly encompassed in the court's thinking. Above all, the court did not want to inhibit attorneys in fulfilling their duty to pursue vigorously their client's interests through the appellate process: "If the issue which the attorney is called upon to decide is fairly debatable, then, under his oath of office, he is not only authorized but obligated to present and urge his client's claim upon the court." Four years earlier, in 1978, in Kirsh v. Duryea (578 P2d 935, Cal, 1978), the court declared: "An attorney is often confronted with clashing obligations imposed by our system of justice. An attorney has an obligation not only to promote his client's interests but also to respect the legitimate interests of fellow members of the Bar, the judiciary, and the administration of justice."

In 1983 a California appellate court in Atchison, Topeka and Santa Fe Railway Co. v. Stockton Port District (140 Cal App3d 111) reversed a trial court's imposition of sanctions for a frivolous action. Here the plaintiff railroad filed a complaint against the public entity seeking damages for failure of a levee which resulted in flooding of railroad property. Admittedly, plaintiff was unsure that the named defendant was the proper defendant, but hoped that discovery would identify the proper defendant. After discovery the complaint was dismissed, and defendant moved for an award of sanctions under the California statute. In reversing the trial court's finding of a frivolous suit, the appellate court pointed out that the lower court had failed to note that the statute of limitations could have barred the suit if plaintiff had not commenced suit at that date, albeit against the wrong defendant. The court did not regard plaintiff's suit as "an action initiated for an improper motive." But in 1984 in In Re Marriage of Gumabao (150 Cal App3d 572) the California Court of Appeals observed that an attorney's actions "constituted tactics which caused unnecessary delay to the opposing party and her counsel" and imposed sanctions upon the attorney:

> Because of Bentson's failure to take the courteous step of notifying Edwards of his predicament, Edwards and his client were required to sit or be available for court the better part of a day. Whether Bentson had a valid excuse or engagement in another trial so as to have a valid defense to contempt is of no consequence to us. His discourteous act towards opposing counsel was not in good faith, was frivolous and caused unnecessary delay and serves as ample justification for being held responsible personally for the attorney's fees of the opposing party. . . .

It should be noted that the court imposed sanctions even though Bentson's actions were not willful, for the court construed the California statute as not requiring willfulness "to be an aspect of the sanctions or tactics." It would appear that the sanctions imposed here were unduly harsh, but justifiably the court must have observed bad faith in the part of the attorney. It is well to note the caveat of the California Supreme Court in In Re Marriage of Flaherty (supra): "Such power in the trial court to grant sanctions upon the court's discretion, unfettered and unbridled, without appropriate safeguards and guidelines could lead to the imposition of sanctions not for misconduct but for forceful advocacy," to which no court would want to be a party.

A variation on the theme of the frivolous appeal is found in the case of Rehler v. Beech Aircraft Corp. (777 F2d 1072, 5th Cir, 1985). Here a pilot died when his ten-year-old aircraft crashed; the investigating federal government agency failed to turn up any malfunctioning parts or mechanical reasons which would have precluded normal operation of the aircraft by the pilot. There was no turbulence and no indication of pilot incapacitation or impairment to operate an aircraft. Nevertheless, the representative plaintiff sued the aircraft manufacturer, charging defective design, failure to warn adequately of the airplane's alleged tendency to spin, and also charging misrepresentations about spin recovery contained in the "Pilot's Operating Handbook." The jury returned a defense verdict stating in response to interrogatories that there was no design defect in the aircraft, no failure by defendant manufacturer to give adequate warnings and instructions, and furthermore that the crash was caused 100 percent by the pilot's own negligence. The pilot's representative appealed on the sole ground that the jury did not consider his argument of misrepresentation with respect to the "Pilot's Operating Handbook." The Fifth U.S. Court of Appeals affirmed, pointing out that the jury's findings were wholly dispositive of the misrepresentation issue; indeed, the interrogatories answered by the jury as well as the judge's charge to the jury were phrased in such a way, according to the court, that, if the jury believed the "Pilot's Operating Handbook" to have misrepresented the spin recovery procedure, the jury would have had to conclude that the defendant had failed to give adequate instructions and adequate warnings, which it did not do. The Fifth U.S. Court of Appeals could have spelled out an almost frivolous appeal, as it found that the misrepresentation count was "sufficiently covered" by the interrogatories and by the instructions to the jury.

The state of New York also has been quite concerned about frivolous appeals: "Undue delay in the prosecution of an appeal tends to frustrate the substantial rights of a respondent," according to Tonkonogy v. Jaffin (249 NYS2d 934, 1st Dept., App Div, 1964). Accordingly, each of the New York Appellate Divisions has provisions in its rules pertaining to the dismissal of appeals for lack of prosecution, nine months generally being determined as the critical time. But in practice the courts have extended this nine-month period, although the courts in New York cannot extend the thirty-day period for serving a notice of appeal under Section 5513 of the New York Civil Practice Law and Rules (CPLR), which is jurisdictional.

1.4 FRIVOLOUS SUBJECTMATTER

Occasionally a taxpayer will allege that because he was involved in some activity for which he could have been criminally prosecuted, he did not file his tax return: in Matz v. U.S. (581 F Supp 714, Ill, 1984) the court deemed his excuse, based upon a Fifth Amendment claim against self-incrimination, to be frivolous within the meaning of the Internal Revenue Code, authorizing imposition of a penalty for filing a frivolous income tax return. Similarly, in Kloes v. U.S. (578 F Supp 270, Wis, 1984), the court found an absence of any specification of legitimate reasons for the particular objections to disclosure of certain income tax information. In Scull v. U.S. (585 F Supp 956, Va, 1984) the taxpayers deducted all of their income as a cost of labor and reported no taxable income; the court deemed the tax return to be "frivolous" and assessed under the Internal Revenue Code a $500 penalty for filing frivolous tax returns.

Where the defendants solicited baseless suits to fight against a competitive shopping center or shopping mall, the court deemed such defenses to be frivolous and therefore dismissible in Landmark Holding Corp. v. Bermant (664 F2d 891, 2nd Cir, 1981).

In Oliveri v. Thompson, decided by the federal district court for the Eastern District of New York on November 13, 1985, Judge Mishler held a lawyer and his indigent client liable for $51,112 in legal fees that Suffolk County had expended in defending what Judge Mishler found was a baseless complaint filed under several civil rights statutes. The client had been arrested in 1982 and charged with offering to sell heroin to a Suffolk County investigator. When the criminal complaint was dropped, the client brought suit in the federal court in 1983 alleging that the officers of Suffolk County had used excessive force in arresting him and had also assaulted him while he was under arrest. The case went to the federal court jury against three officers, and the jury found that there was probable cause for his arrest, that there was no excessive force or assault, and that the felony complaint was not maliciously signed because the arresting officers were acting under a good faith belief. Judge Mishler observed that the claims were "instituted without any factual basis whatsoever . . . devoid of any factual basis." Accordingly, the attorney and his client were liable for counsel fees and costs for "instituting meritless claims and for continuing the prosecution of claims after it became apparent that they were without a factual or legal basis."

The divorce situation is especially conducive to frivolous actions, as illustrated by Gabrelian v. Gabrelian in the New York Appellate Division, 2nd Dept., dated May 20, 1985. Here the defendant husband moved pro se to punish his wife for contempt for allegedly failing to comply with provisions of the divorce decree. The lower court found no contumacious conduct on the part of the wife, and noted that the husband had instituted unsuccessfully three prior proceedings seeking indentical relief. Finding that the husband's conduct was "harassing and vexatious," the lower court imposed a $500 fine upon him, payable to his former wife, and the husband filed the appeal. The appellate court observed that

> there is an inherent power vested in all courts of record in this State to regulate and control the conduct of litigants and counsel appearing before such courts, and, further, the specific power to impose financial sanctions upon a party or attorney who has engaged in abusive litigations practices.

However, the appellate court found that the $500 fine "constituted an improvident exercise of discretion" and reversed the lower court, and opined:

> It may well be that the time has come for courts, pursuant to their inherent powers (see, also, Judson v. Three D. Bldg Corp., 18 AD 2d 232, 236; 20 Am Jur 2d, Courts, §§78, 79), to impose sanctions upon parties and/or their attorneys who frustrate the expeditious disposition of appropriate litigated matters by engaging in dilatory or frivolous conduct during the course of litigation calculated to impede the orderly administration of justice and cast an undue burden on the Judges and their supporting staff (see W. Freedman and Brown, The Frivolous Suit and Frivolous Defense, NYLJ, Dec. 4, 1979, p. 1, col 2, for an extended discussion of the issues touched upon herein). The court should, therefore, have available to it options such as the terms sought by plaintiff herein to encourage due regard and concern for the sanctity of the judicial process. . . . The question of whether the inherent power is to be invoked in a particular case must be determined on an ad hoc basis; the court must determine, in its discretion, whether a monetary assessment would be just and fair, and whether its imposition would be consistent with sound policy considerations, e.g., promoting speedy, efficient and inexpensive resolution of lawsuits, on their merits, and deterring neglect, delay and intentional abuse such as the institution of successive baseless and frivolous legal proceedings that

serve no purpose other than harassment and that hinder the courts from acting upon more meritorious claims. Because inherent powers are not subject to direct democratic controls, they must be invoked with great restraint, as there is a danger that such powers might be wielded arbitrarily or in doubtful cases. . . . Finally, we hold that the court may, in its discretion, invoke its inherent power to require an abusive or neglectful litigant or attorney to pay a sum of money to the opposing party, when such party has suffered by reason of the abusive conduct; alternatively, the judge may direct that such payment be made directly to the court, when it appears that the efficient disposition of the business before it has been impaired by reason of the conduct in question.

The concurring opinion of the court was equally important:

Despite this strong public policy of encouraging and ensuring open and unimpeded access to the courts, the majority of my colleagues have concluded that there exists an immense and undefined inherent judicial power, seemingly bounded only by constitutional restraints, to impose unspecified monetary sanctions upon attorneys or litigants who engage in conduct which is deemed by a particular judge to be abusive or negligent, such as filing a frivolous lawsuit or appeal or making a meritless motion. The determination of just what type of conduct warrants the imposition of a sanction, the amount of the sanction, whether it is to be imposed on the attorney or the litigant, and whether it is to be paid to the court or the opposing party must of necessity be left largely to the discretion of the individual judge. No limitation is placed upon the amount of the sanction, no clear guidelines are established for its exercise, and only the vaguest suggestions as to appropriate procedural safeguards are made. Thus, by a simple act of jurisprudential legerdemain, my colleagues have sidestepped the many restrictions normally imposed upon procedures tending to limit access to the courts and effectively rendered the statutory and common law restrictions mere precatory admonitions. . . . No longer will a defendant who feels he has unjustly been sued be limited to recover damages for malicious prosecution of abuse of process, despite an unbroken line of precedent holding that these are his only remedies. Rather, he need merely persuade a judge that the case is frivolous and he may then request the imposition of sanctions to recompense him for his losses. Moreover, such damages may be assessed against an attorney who has acted negligently, despite the well-settled rule that "when baseless legal proceedings are instituted by a lawyer on behalf of a client, the courts have not recognized any liability of the lawyer to third parties therefore where the factual situations have not fallen within one of the acknowledged categories of tort or contract liability."

Also troubling is the fact that frivolity, like beauty, is often in the eyes of the beholder. An action or motion which may appear frivolous to one judge may in fact be the beginning of a new development in the law. Many causes of action and procedures which are commonplace today would at one time have been deemed frivolous. For example, prior to the swift demise of the citadel of privity (see Codling v. Paglia, 32 NY 2d 330, 338-339) and the dramatic growth of a cause of action in strict products liability (compare Escola v. Coca Cola Bottling Co., 24 Cal 2d 453, 150 P 2d 436, with Greenman v. Yuba Power Products, Inc., 59 Cal 2d 57, 377 P 2d 897), cases asserting such claims might well have been deemed frivolous. Another such example is the cause of action for negligent infliction of emotional harm, which has only recently found limited acceptance by the Court of Appeals (see Bovsun v. Sanperi, 61 NY 2d 219). In a similar vein, prior to Dole v. Dow Chem. Co. (30 NY 2d 143), a claim for contribution by an active tort-feasor would have been considered nonsensical (see, e.g., Jackson v. Associated Dry Goods Corp., 13 NY 2d 112). Indeed, the day is not long past when a claim that a woman was entitled to choose to have an abortion, that a couple was entitled to a certain degree of sexual privacy, or that a person had a right to attend an integrated public school would have been summarily rejected. Yet it is as a result of the constant influx of novel claims, innovative procedures and fresh ideas that our common law grows and flourishes. Without them, it must inevitably stultify and decay.

1.5 DISCOVERY ABUSES

While the frivolous lawsuit, the frivolous answer, the frivolous appeal, and the frivolous subjectmatter have played significant roles in the ever-present problem of expediting justly the litigation system, the area of discovery has been particularly noted for the wealth of abuses that has permeated it. Excessive discovery is but one aspect of the abusive conduct and irresponsible behavior on the party of counsel and their clients that courts must face. In Berkey Photo Inc. v. Eastman Kodak Co. (74 FRD 613, SDNY, 1977) counsel did not produce copies of documents that had been requested at pre-trial until the very end of the trial, even though the attorney knew that the documents had not been destroyed as he had stated. Judge Leval in Stillwagon v. New Jersey Transit Rail Operations, Inc., on December 23, 1985, imposed discovery sanctions for failure to produce documents in accordance with a prior order of the federal district court for the Southern District of New York; his preclusion order took the facts as established by the opposing side and also awarded the opposing side $1,000 in costs. In Penthouse International, Ltd. v. Playboy Enterprises, Inc. (86 FRD 396, SDNY, 1980; aff 663 F2d 371, 2nd Cir, 1981) the willful misconduct of the plaintiff in failing to comply with the discovery process led the court to dismiss the complaint. When the defense attorney in Paris v. Waterman Steamship Corp., decided January 30, 1986, by the New York Supreme Court, New York County, produced at trial unauthorized medical files which he falsely stated had been furnished to him by plaintiff's counsel, the New York court struck the answer and ordered an immediate assessment of damages in the seaman's personal injury action. Terming the episode that touched off a mistrial "an abuse of discovery," the court pointed to the fact that the litigation was "about thirteen years old" and was "a kind of close-to-the-vest gamemanship and the kind of playmanship that should have no place in serious litigation."

In U.S. v. American Telephone & Telegraph Co. (86 FRD 603, DC, 1979) the court observed that the defendant had asked for 500,000 documents which discovery request was later pared down to 35,000 documents: "Frivolous resistance to legitimate discovery requests must be curtailed if justice is to be done."

Discovery abuse is said to exist because some litigation is itself abusive, as witness the unwelcome class action based on few facts. (See 44 *Antitrust Law Journal* 14, 1975). Then the cost of commencing the discovery is nominal compared with the latter gains to be enjoyed, even in settlement; in *forma pauperis* litigation, for example, costs nothing, à la Section 1915(a) of Title 28 of U.S. Code: "Any court of the United States may authorize the commencement . . . of any suit, action, or proceeding, civil or criminal . . . without prepayment of fees and costs . . . by a person who makes affidavit that he is unable to pay such costs or give security therefor." The low rates of prejudgment interest awarded in federal courts also militate in favor of commencing suit and tackling extensive discovery. Discovery abuse is a vital part and parcel of the entire process, nourished by the 1983 intention of the drafters of the Federal Rules of Civil Procedure (FRCP) to encourage very broad discovery (15 *Tennessee Law Review* 737, 1939). In fact, it was contemplated by the FRCP drafters that anything remotely relevant would be discoverable, particularly if it would lead to admissible evidence. The thrust was to seek the truth and not to be encumbered by procedures that frustrated that noble purpose. (See Martin v. Reynolds Metals Corp., 297 F2d 49, 9th Cir, 1961.) In Hickman v. Taylor (329 US 495, 1947) the U.S. Supreme Court, while cautioning against "fishing expeditions," nevertheless declared that "discovery is available in all types of cases at the behest of any party, individual or corporate, plaintiff or defendant. . . . civil trials in the federal courts no longer need be carried on in the dark." But the District of Columbia Court of Appeals in United Presbyterian Church v. Reagan (738 F2d 1375, 1984) construed a "fishing expedition . . . undertaken in the hope that some cause of action might be uncovered" as a fairly common example of discovery abuse.

Discovery abuse is also traceable to the fact that unsuccessful litigants are not responsible for payment of their opposing attorneys' fees (Roadway Express, Inc. v. Piper, 447 US 752, 1980). Thus, unnecessary discovery is cheap, and the requested party must assume the enormous costs of collecting, organizing, duplicating, and delivering requested documents and papers, all at the cost of the party from whom the documents and papers are solicited in the discovery process. The costs may be shifted to the requesting party where it is shown that bad faith permeated the entire discovery proceeding (see 40 *Fordham Law Review* 761, 1972), although such an outcome is dependent upon specific statutory authority such as Rule 56(g) of the Federal Rules of Civil Procedure, which permits federal courts to impose attorneys' fees and costs also in bad faith litigation. Mr. Justice Lewis F. Powell of the U.S. Supreme Court in U.S. v. American Telephone & Telegraph Co. (supra) observed that "all too often discovery practices enable the party with the greatest financial resources to prevail by exhausting the resources of a weaker opponent." The Litigation Section of the American Bar Association in its January 1981 report, "Report of the Discovery Committee's Subcommittee on Pretrial Litigation Ethics and Practices," concluded:

[L]itigated discovery contests have become so commonplace that it is difficult to distinguish between the zealous, ethically correct attorneys and those who are misusing the procedure to harass, annoy, and create litigation expenses to force the opposing party into an unfavorable compromise of a legitimate claim or defense or to obtain tactical advantages from the delay and costs of the contest.

Massive discovery involving great social issues and complex political problems like the monopoly issue taken up in U.S. v. American Telephone & Telegraph Co. (642 F2d 1285, DC Cir, 1980) generates tremendous costs as both sides press to uncover every issue whether salient or not; and therein lie opportunities for great abuses, as perhaps illustrated by Blue Chip Stamps Co. v. Manor Drug Stores, Inc. (421 US 723, 1985), where the U.S. Supreme Court refused to grant the relief requested because there were great opportunities for discovery abuse in securities litigation that could frustrate normal business activity. Here plaintiff who allegedly relied on misleading statements in a company's prospectus, resulting in a lost opportunity to purchase stock, sought to bring the action under Rule 10b-5 of the Securities and Exchange Act (SEC). The court was mindful of the precedent that would be established if full trials were required for every potential plaintiff or plaintiffs.

The inclination of both sides to equalize discovery costs also contributes to discovery abuse as each side tries to outdo the other, and perhaps in the final analysis to deter more excessive discovery requests. Since lawyers generally bill on the hourly basis, the incentive to excessive discovery is implicitly understood and recognized by bench and bar.

The Texas Supreme Court in Downer v. Aquamarine Operators Inc., on December 4, 1985, upheld the power of the trial court to strike a party's pleading as a sanction for failing to produce witnesses for oral depositions. Here plaintiff had instituted a wrongful death action for the death of her husband, and the trial court had granted her a interlocutory default judgment when defendant failed to produce witnesses for the depositions.

On occasion, discovery abuses simply do not result, even though plaintiff's discovery pursuits may appear to be highly anomalous. In Roberts v. Carrier Corp. (107 FRD 678 ND Ind, 1985), for example, the plaintiff was injured when his house caught fire allegedly due to a defect in the furnace; he sought by way of discovery information relating to the manufacture of the furnace, its component parts, and especially the gas control valve. Plaintiff who commenced his case in Texas pursued the non-defendant gas valve manufacturer into Indiana; at the ancillary proceedings the non-defendant defended against the discovery demand by stating that the requested information had been furnished to the Consumer Product Safety Commission (CPSC) in Washington, D.C., and that the non-defendant had a common law privilege against disclosing "critical self-analysis." The federal district court agreed with the non-defendant that the non-defendant "is entitled to assert the privilege over that portion of the documents which was prepared for the CPSC and which contains self-critical analysis.''

To curb discovery abuses former U.S. Supreme Court Justice Arthur Goldberg, writing in the *American Bar Association Journal* (February 1986) at pp. 39-40, argued that oral discovery should be eliminated because it causes ''undue delay, burdens an overworked judiciary, is largely ineffective and contributes substantially to the ever-growing expense of litigation.'' Justice Goldberg then opined:

> A notorious example of abuse of discovery is United States v. AT&T, 642 F2d 1285 (D.C. Cir, 1980). This important lawsuit involved 11 years of discovery. Ma Bell and the Justice Department undoubtedly can bear the enormous expenses of protracted discovery. Most litigants faced with such a prospect would sensibly throw in the towel.

He then observed that ''the judiciary appears to be very reluctant to impose the sanctions mandated (by the Federal Rules of Civil Procedure)'':

> One reason is that judges feel that sanctions create an atmosphere of hostility rather than of cooperation in the conduct of litigation. But a more basic reason is that all judges, in their earlier years, were at the bar and consequently imbued with the discovery mystique. In light of the failure of sanctions to correct discovery abuses, it is my considered view that the only remedy is to eliminate the deposing of witnesses.

Former Justice Goldberg then proposed the following reforms, to wit:

1. Deposition of a witness should be permitted only where, upon motion, there appears to be a reasonable likelihood that the witness will be unavailable for testimony at trial.
2. A limited number of written interrogatories should be permitted. I emphasize limited, because written interrogatories too, if unchecked, can be the subject of great abuse. This already is recognized by some local court rules that drastically limit the number of written interrogatories.
3. A complete exchange of written documents on both sides that are proposed to be introduced in evidence should be mandated.
4. Each party to civil litigation should be required to furnish the other side with a definitive list of proposed witnesses. This is provided for in some local rules, but should be required in all civil litigation.

It is obvious that discovery abuses account for considerable litigation expense and costly delay; indeed, justice delayed is justice denied.

2

The Medical and Dental Malpractice Entanglement

2.1 PROFESSIONAL MALPRACTICE

Professional persons like physicians and dentists as well as those who undertake any health care work calling for special skill and experience are generally required not only to exercise reasonable care in what they do but also to possess the minimum standard of special knowledge and ability. In malpractice litigation today, physicians and surgeons top the list (see 12 *Vanderbilt Law Review* 549, 1959), followed by dentists (Le Beuf v. Atkins, 621 P2d 787, Wash, 1981), pharmacists (Troppi v. Scarf, 187 NW2d 511, Mich, 1971), psychiatrists (Weatherly v. State of New York, 441 NYS2d, 319, 1981), and other health care professions. The medical and dental practitioner does not contract to cure a patient, nor does he warrant or assure either a correct diagnosis or a successful course of treatment (Stanley v. Fisher, 417 NE2d 932, Ind, 1981). Accordingly, the physician and dentist are generally not liable for an honest mistake of judgment. But by undertaking to perform the medical or dental service, the professional practitioner is ordinarily understood to hold himself out as having standard professional skill and knowledge, even when his services are done gratuitously (Sullivan v. Henry, 287 SE2d 652, Ga, 1981). Thus, the doctor and dentist must have and must use the knowledge, skill, and care ordinarily possessed and employed by members in good standing of the medical and dental professions, respectively (Young v. Park, 417 A2d 889, RI, 1980). This knowledge, skill, and care is generally quantified as the knowledge, skill, and care of the "average" member of the respective professional community in good standing, as described in Green v. United States (530 F Supp 633, Wis, 1982). Where the doctor or dentist represents himself as a specialist, he is required to possess a higher knowledge, skill, and care (Coyne v. Cirilli, 607 P2d 1383, Ore, 1980).

The professional practitioner in the medical and dental fields is also entitled to be judged according to the tenets of the professional school that he professes to follow (Roberts v. Tardif, 417 A2d 444, Me, 1980). The professional standard of the local medical or dental community is also a factor in judging his liability (King v. Williams, 279 SE2d 618, SC, 1981), although many courts favor a general national standard, as shown in Shilkret v. Annapolis Emergency Hospital Assn. (349 A2d 245, MD, 1975).

Negligence on the part of the medical or dental practitioner is generally based upon and proved by expert testimony, as illustrated in Cross v. Huttenlocher (440 A2d 952, Conn, 1981): "To prevail in a malpractice case the plaintiff must establish through expert testimony both the standard of care and the fact that the defendant's conduct did not measure up to that standard." But some courts have permitted circumstantial evidence and even the common knowledge of laymen to attest to professional negligence where the facts of the case are not within the medical or dental technology, such as a surgeon cutting off the wrong leg or the dentist extracting the wrong tooth. (See Steinke v. Bell, 107 A2d 825, NJ, 1954.)

In general, the medical and dental professions are unique among most skilled professions in that the very practitioners charged with negligence make the rules and regulations and set their own legal standards of conduct as to what constitutes "good practice." In Toth v. Community Hospital (292 NYS2d 440, 1968) the New York Court of Appeals had occasion to remark: "The law generally permits the medical [and dental] profession to establish its own standard of care." But "if a physician fails to employ his expertise or best judgment, and that omission causes injury, he should not automatically be freed from liability because in fact he adhered to acceptable practice." In December 1985 the New York Appellate Division, 1st Dept., in Alvarez v. Prospect Hospital, had occasion to apply the holding of the Toth case (supra). Here plaintiff's cancerous condition allegedly went untreated for a year after plaintiff was diagnosed as suffering from acute gastroenteritis. One year later, after the abdominal pain continued, the same radiologist conducted new tests that again showed intestinal cancer but apparently took no action other than routinely forwarding the results to the attending physician who had ordered the x-rays and other tests. The court opined:

> Applying the Toth holding to the instant case, we find that Dr. Stark was more than simply an x-ray technician, and as a consequence of that fact, we conclude that there is an issue of fact as to the extent of the duty he owed to plaintiff. . . . There are too many questions unanswered at this time relative to the standard of care, if any, that defendant owed to plaintiff relative to subsequent treatment.

The dissenting justices maintained that the radiologist "clearly demonstrated adequate medical conduct" because his sole medical function "was to read and interpret the film'' and he did not have a professional responsibility in the ''care and treatment of this plaintiff.'' The dissenters were angry because the court was

> holding professional people responsible for their malpractice and permitting those who have performed their tasks in a satisfactory manner to be insulated from the expense and personal burden of having to defend lawsuits which have no foundation.

The dissenters also objected to allowing plaintiffs

> to use a vacuum cleaner to suck in each and every physician, no matter how tangential his relationship to the patient, as a defendant, even where the facts clearly demonstrate adequate medical conduct. . . . in time, we won't have any physicians at all to treat the ill.

The late 1960s and early 1970s witnessed a tremendous increase in the volume of medical and dental malpractice actions, both in the size of the verdicts and/or judgments and in the cost of medical or dental insurance coverage. The ''crisis'' precipitated, inter alia, the frivolous lawsuit designed to force the professional defendants and their malpractice insurance carriers to settle cases, perhaps by payment for ''nuisance value'' or to ''blackmail'' the defendants into payment to avoid the publicity of a malpractice suit. These picayune lawsuits occupied the attention of bench and bar as well as insurance carriers, and several remedies have been proposed, to wit: (1) the losing plaintiff or claimant can be made to pay attorney's fees, the costs of the action, and interest thereon, to the successful defending doctor or dentist or hospital; *or* (2) the doctor or dentist posits a counterclaim, or countersues the attorney and the patient, and seeks to collect substantial damages. The New York Appellate Division, 1st Dept., on February 24, 1986, in Doody v. Booth Memorial Hospital struck out the affirmative defenses including contributory negligence because it found that decedent's estate, or plaintiff, herein alleged ''culpable conduct'' was a ''sham'':

> From their own records, the physicians and hospital personnel involved must know where and when plaintiff failed to give a complete and accurate medical history or failed to follow advice or instructions. Yet they allege that they need discovery to respond. Though not required to provide evidence, defendants' bills of particular provide facts in amplification of the defense. It will not do in these circumstances to claim that the facts will be provided after discovery.

Here the decedent, age thirty-four, had gone to the hospital at the direction of a physician who was ''covering'' for her regular physician. Within several hours after being sent back to her home, the decedent was brought to another hospital by emergency ambulance where she and the baby died after her uterus ruptured.

2.2 THE SUCCESSFUL PRACTITIONER

In Peerman v. Sidicane (605 SW2d 242, 1980) the Tennessee Court of Appeals observed that a female patient had filed a complaint against the physician for negligently diagnosing her ailment as gonorrhea. The patient alleged that she suffered mental anguish because the physician had delayed the test results from a medical laboratory until he had obtained a "kickback" from the laboratory. The trial court granted summary judgment in favor of the physician, finding that the physician had, in fact, informed her after a physical examination that she *might* have gonorrhea, but seven days later had in fact told her that the tests revealed *no* gonorrhea. Suit for malicious prosecution was thereupon instituted by the doctor against the patient and her attorney, who apparently had made no effort to ascertain the facts of the case. Her attorney did not interview any physicians regarding the standard of care, nor had he taken any depositions in the malpractice suit. Furthermore, the attorney had no knowledge as to whether the physician was or was not involved in a kickback situation. (The attorney merely surmised that a kickback might be involved.) The Tennessee jury returned an $11,500 verdict in favor of the physician ($3,000 compensatory damages and $8,500 punitive damages). The jury believed that the patient's attorney had entered, without his client's consent, allegations in the complaint based upon pure speculation and had maliciously prosecuted the physician.

Another successful countersuit by a physician was Raine v. Drasin (621 SW2d 895, 1981), decided by the Kentucky Court of Appeals. The original plaintiff was a cardiac patient whose shoulder was injured while he was hospitalized. Suit was brought against the radiologist and orthopedist, seeking a total of $1 million in damages. But weeks later the suit was dismissed with prejudice by the patient because it was then clear that the injury occurred before the two doctors came on the scene. Thereupon, these two physicians sued the two attorneys for the plaintiff, as well as the plaintiff-patient, for malicious prosecution. The jury returned verdicts in the amount of $37,500 compensatory and punitive damages against the first attorney, and $12,500 in compensatory damages against the second attorney. The Kentucky Court of Appeals ruled that the initial malpractice suit had been properly terminated in favor of the two doctors, but the court found reputational damage had been suffered by the two physicians because of the libelous statements in the complaint of the initial action. On the issue of malice, the court agreed that the first attorney who drafted the complaint had acted maliciously because he was aware of the lack of any probable cause to sue these physicians. Furthermore, there was "evidence indicating that [Raine's] motivation may have been to obtain discovery against the hospital by suing the [physicians] rather than by employing the proper means of discovery." This inference was sufficient to permit the jury to believe that Raine had acted from improper and unlawful motives, tantamount to malice. (Note that the first attorney had another hospital as a client and therefore had not even signed the complaint here.) The Kentucky Supreme Court dismissed the punitive damages award, thereby reducing the award of compensatory damages to $15,000 against the first attorney only.

The Nevada Supreme Court in Bull v. McCuskey (615 P2d 957, 1980) found that an elderly patient had developed bedsores while under a doctor's care; that the attending physician was promptly dismissed and replaced by another doctor; and that although the second doctor told the patient's nephew that there was no malpractice, the nephew nevertheless instituted suit against the first physician. The court approved an award of damages against the attorney for abuse of process because the attorney had "the ulterior motive of coercing a nuisance settlement." The court pointed out that the attorney had taken no deposition of the physician, had conferred with no other doctor, and during the trial called the defendant physician an "incompetent, a fumble-fingered fellow, a liar, a scoundrel, a damned idiot. . . . It will be a cold day in hell when I let that dum-dum take care of my mother."

The Kansas Supreme Court in Nelson v. Miller (607 P2d 438, 1980) reversed a trial court's dismissal of a physician's suit against attorneys who had filed a malpractice action against him:

> [T]he attorney must accept the obligation to conduct a reasonable investigation in an attempt to find what the true facts are before filing a civil action on behalf of his client. In determining probable cause in a malicious prosecution action brought against an attorney, a jury may properly consider not only those facts disclosed to counsel by the client but also those facts which could have been learned by a diligent effort on the attorney's part. In determining the purpose of the attorney in filing a civil action, a jury may properly consider as evidence of good faith or absence of malice the fact that the attorney before filing an action, made a demand upon his client's adversary and extended to him the opportunity to respond with his version of the facts. This should be the standard procedure unless an immediate filing of an action is required by the imminent running of the statute of limitations or some other good reason.

According to 27 *Loyola Law Review* 325 (1981), when a wrongful malpractice suit is filed in the state of Louisiana and allegedly harms a physician (through the fault of an attorney), the physician should be able to sue the attorney successfully under Article 2315 of the Louisiana Civil Code, which does not require "malice" but only "fault" upon which to base the countersuit: "There is fault when a person's conduct has not been that of a normally careful, attentive, and diligent man, in short, that of a prudent person."

2.3 THE UNSUCCESSFUL PRACTITIONER

The majority view is against the physician or professional practitioner in instituting the retaliatory suit against the attorney or his client, and there are indeed more unsuccessful efforts than successful ones. In the case of Tappen

v. Ager (559 F2d 376, 10th Cir, 1979), Dr. Ager brought an obstetrical malpratice and wrongful death action against Dr. Tappen for the latter's alleged misconduct at the birth of Dr. Ager's daughter. Without waiting for the disposition of these cases, Dr. Tappen brought a countersuit alleging, among other theories of liability, that Dr. Ager himself was negligent in failing to adequately investigate the suit prior to filing it, and was therefore guilty of abuse of process. The trial court dismissed Dr. Tappen's countersuit, and Dr. Tappen appealed. The federal court, applying Kansas law, affirmed the trial court's judgment, and held that there is no recognizable negligence tort which arises from merely prosecuting a lawsuit since there is no duty running from plaintiff to defendant to use reasonable care in filing a suit. The court further found that abuse of process was inapplicable since there was no ulterior purpose in filing the malpractice action. The court also rejected Dr. Tappen's other counts and concluded that there is no actionable tort based upon the intentional filing of litigation without merit; and that the filing of a suit, if free from malice, is privileged from liability for invasion of privacy. This is indeed the majority view in the United States today.

The Michigan Supreme Court in Friedman v. Dozoroc (312 NW2d 585, 1981) analyzed carefully the suit by a urologist who sued two attorneys after a medical malpractice claim against the urologist had been dismissed. Dr. Friedman's countersuit was based upon abuse of process, malicious prosecution, and negligence. The defendant attorneys had evidently filed the malpractice claim without being able to produce an expert medical witness, according to Dr. Friedman's lawyer. They represented the husband of a patient who had undergone routine bladder surgery by Dr. Friedman, and the woman had died on the operating table without apparent cause, but an autopsy later revealed that her death was caused by a rare blood condition (thrombocytopenic purpura) that is not diagnosable and is uniformly fatal. Despite their knowledge of the autopsy report, the attorneys still brought the claim against Dr. Friedman. Dr. Friedman's case against the lawyers was dismissed at the trial court level; however, the Michigan Court of Appeals ruled that he had a cause of action for malicious prosecution (Friedman v. Dozoroc and Golden, 83 Mich App 429, 1978). Dr. Friedman's lawyer in the countersuit was heard to say: "To an increasing degree, lawyers are going to be held responsible for their acts just like everyone else. These guys are proud of being hired guns, yet they're allowed to walk down the street and willy-nilly shoot anybody in sight." Both sides appealed to the Michigan Supreme Court, and the highest state court ruled that the patient's attorneys owed no actionable duty to the plaintiff physician, and therefore the attorneys were not subject to liability for negligent conduct. The creation of an attorney's duty in favor of an adversary would be an unacceptable conflict of interest which could seriously hamper the attorney's effectiveness as counsel for his client as well as for access to courts. The Michigan Supreme Court pointed out that to recover upon the theory of abuse of process, plaintiff must prove "ulterior purpose" or an "irregular act"; and on the malicious prosecution action the court reversed and found no proof of "special injury" (which requirement the dissenters would abolish). The decision was close, 4-3, and Justice Levin, who wrote the majority opinion for four justices, had to write on his own a concurring opinion joined in by one justice; there were two dissenting opinions in which one more justice concurred. (The majority opinion had noticed that the original malpractice suit had been filed almost two years after the death of the patient, who died five days after surgery from "a rare and uniformly fatal blood disease, the cause and cure of which are unknown.")

The Illinois Appellate Court in Stopka v. Lesser (402 NE2d 781, 1980) affirmed the dismissal of the physician's malicious prosecution case against the patient's attorney. It seems that the patient was treated badly in the emergency room of the hospital, and a medical malpractice suit was filed against the hospital and a treating physician. Five months later, in an amended complaint, an inactive physician on the hospital staff was named as an additional defendant. This inactive physician was obviously not involved in the treatment of the patient, and it was not until years later that the patient's attorney dismissed the inactive physician from the lawsuit. The inactive physician thereupon sued for damage to his reputation, mental anguish, and increased cost of insurance premiums. He alleged that the patient's attorney had breached a duty to him, thereby causing these damages. The trial court dismissed the suit upon the ground that the attorney owed no recognized legal duty to the inactive physician. The Illinois appellate court in affirming the dismissal pointed out that the inactive physician did not sustain a *special* injury beyond that of defending a malpractice lawsuit! However, the court indicated that it favored a reassessment of the "special damages" issued in Illinois so as to "impose a meaningful duty upon attorneys to ascertain whether the party sued is possibly liable for the wrong committed." The court expressed the opinion that Illinois should "effectively deter meritless litigation by providing recovery from the attorney to the victim without the requirement of special damages."

The Indiana Court of Appeals in Wong v. Taylor (422 NE2d 1279, 1981) sent an ominous message to physicians contemplating retaliatory legal action. Here Dr. Wong hospitalized Mrs. Privett to determine the cause of her persistent headaches and later referred her to a sinus specialist. Months later on her own Mrs. Privett underwent surgery for an anterior cervical fusion and ended up as a quadraplegic. After surgery Dr. Wong in the hospital had prescribed mineral oil for her, but had not rendered any pre-operative treatment or post-operative treatment; he had not even referred Mrs. Privett to the surgeon. Nevertheless, the present defendant lawyer for Mrs. Privett instituted a malpractice action against Dr. Wong two years thereafter. A summary judgment in favor of Dr. Wong occurred almost two years later, at which time Dr. Wong retaliated with a malicious prosecution suit against the patient's attorney. (Dr. Wong's medical malpractice insurance premiums had by then increased 30 percent and his total income decreased.) In 1979, almost three years later, the jury awarded Dr. Wong $25,000, which amount was set aside by the court, and the

Indiana appellate court concurred that Dr. Wong had failed to prove malicious prosecution, i.e., the element of probable cause. The court ruled that present defendant attorney had probable cause to sue Dr. Wong based on the facts known to him when the suit was commenced.

The New York Court of Appeals in Drago v. Buonagurio (386 NE2d 821, 1978) added a new dimension to the retaliatory suit by the unsuccessful physician by observing that

> [w]hatever may be the constraints imposed by the Code of Professional Responsibility with the associated sanctions of professional discipline when baseless legal proceedings are instituted by a lawyer on behalf of a client, the courts have not recognized any liability of the lawyer to third parties thereof where the factual situations have not fallen within one of the acknowledged categories of tort or contract liability.

It might be similarly pointed out that physicians who sought relief on the novel theory of a ''prima facie tort,'' i.e., ''the infliction of an intentional harm without excuse or justification by an act or series of acts which otherwise would be lawful and which results in special damages'' (Martin v. Trevino, 578 SW2d 763, Tex, 1978), have been generally unsuccessful. Even where it is argued that a failure to recognize the ''prima facie tort'' infringes upon the constitutional guarantee of a remedy for every wrong, the courts have refused to accept the physician's argument, as illustrated by Belsky v. Lowenthal (392 NE2d 560, NY, 1979).

The injustice in not permitting the countersuit is aptly illustrated by O'Toole v. Franklin (569 P2d 561, Ore, 1977). Here a patient sued two physicians, alleging that he had been given a medication which caused damage to his hearing. But the truth of the matter was that the physicians had not seen the patient until after the medication had been discontinued, and so they notified plaintiff's attorney that they could not have played any role in the alleged injury. But the attorney ignored their requests to have the complaint dismissed. Finally, six months later the court on motion dismissed the complaint, and the two physicians commenced a countersuit based upon the substantial adverse publicity and adverse coverage by the news media: ''loss of professional reputation is a special injury that is not an ordinary result of litigation. . . . defamatory matter asserting incompetency to conduct one's profession is libelous per se and requires no proof of special injury. Damages are presumed.'' But the Oregon Supreme Court readily disposed of their argument and dismissed the countersuit on the ground that harm to reputation arising from an unfounded charge of malpractice is not the ''special injury'' required for imposing liability for malicious prosecution.

It is well to note the 1897 words of the North Dakota Supreme Court in Kolka v. Jones (71 NW 565):

The malicious prostitution of legal remedies to observe unworthy personal ends is not only an injury to the victim of the particular persecution, but also to society at large, if it is suffered to go unwhipped of justice. If the law will not punish such conduct, public confidence in the merits of our system of jurisprudence must inevitably be shaken, and the courts themselves will seem to have forsaken their high function as protectors and vindicators of invaded rights and to have become, instead, the accomplices of evil men.

Dental malpractice, while pale by comparison with the volume and exorbitant cost of medical malpractice, has grown dramatically in recent years. As dentistry becomes more and more sophisticated, and as the consumer-patient becomes more aware of malpractice "opportunities" for windfall financial returns, the exposure of the dentist to malpractice is taken for granted. The more highly specialized is the dental professional, the higher the standard of care is required, as delineated in Section 299A of Restatement (Second) of Torts, Comment d. Dental malpractice rests upon a finding of fault, and strict liability is generally not applied to the breach of duty of care by the professional (Kent v. Henson, 330 SE2d 126, Ga App, 1985). In addition to common law negligence standards, state dental licensing statutes typically provide a standard of due care; see In Re Proposed Disciplinary Action Against the Dentist License of Schultz (375 NW2d 509, Minn, 1985).

The dentist is "not an insurer or warrantor that the exercise of his professional judgment will effect a cure of the patient. Nor is he obliged to bring to the exercise of his profession the utmost skill: if he measures up to the qualifications and applies the reasonable care and skill legally required by the Code, he is not responsible for a mistake in judgment" (Kent v. Henson, supra).

Both medical and dental malpractice have generated what the *New York Times* described as "a real nasty fight" with the legal profession (February 14, 1986, at p. A18): "The doctors say fee-hungry lawyers are filing too many suits against them. The lawyers say there are too many incompetent doctors." A bumper sticker proposed by one doctor's wife would read "Support your lawyer. Send your child to medical school." Most of the thunder has come from plaintiffs' lawyers' organization, the 65,000 member Association of Trial Lawyers of America, but the conservative American Bar Association has recently entered the fray to effect balance. The newly formed American Tort Reform Association embraces among its members the American Medical Association, the American Association of Community and Junior Colleges, as well as such business groups as the National Paint and Coatings Association; its president, a former Pennsylvania congressman, calls plaintiff-trial lawyers "vultures." The February 19, 1986, decision of the New York Court of Appeals in Hill v. St. Clare's Hospital should give the American Tort Reform Association an enormous headache: here the highest New York court ruled that a physician who operates a medical clinic in New York City may be held vicariously liable for the malpractice of a treating doctor, even though the owner-physician neither participated in nor controlled the diagnosis of the particular plaintiff-patient nor the treatment prescribed. Part of the difficulty was the release given to an original tortfeasor, and the court ruled that this issue would be remanded for hearings under Section 4533-b of the New York Civil Practice Law and Rules (CPLR).

3

Abuse of Process

3.1 NATURE OF THE CAUSE OF ACTION

Where legal procedure or process has been set in motion in proper form, with probable cause, but has been perverted to accomplish an ulterior motive for which the legal procedure or process was not designed, the tort of abuse of process occurs. (See Section 682 of Restatement (Second) of Torts.) A fitting example is set forth in Board of Education v. Farmingdale Classroom Teachers Assn. (380 NYS2d 635, 1975), which involved a bitter dispute between the parties culminating in the defendant being charged with violation of the New York anti-strike law. A hearing was scheduled to determine culpability, and defendant subpoenaed eighty-seven teachers to appear on the first day of the hearing, although the plaintiff had requested that the teachers' appearances be staggered to relieve the burden on the school district. To avoid a shutdown of the school system plaintiff was forced to hire a great number of substitute teachers. Plaintiff then brought suit for abuse of process, and the trial court refused to dismiss the complaint; the New York Court of Appeals agreed that an abuse of process action may be maintained even by a party who was not the recipient of the process or subpoena, because there was a misuse or perversion of regularly issued legal process for an improper purpose, to wit: the shutdown of the school system. Judge Sol Wachtler set forth the three essential elements of the abuse of process action: (1) there must be a regularly issued process; (2) the motivation behind the process must be unjustifiable harm or damage to another; and (3) the party issuing the process must be seeking an advantage for himself or a detriment to the plaintiff which is outside the legitimate ends or purposes of the process.

In Brody v. Ruby (267 NW2d 902, Iowa, 1978) abuse of process was defined as "misuse or perversion of regularly issued legal process, after it has been issued, to achieve some collateral purpose not justified by the nature of the process." Thus, no liability will be predicated where the process was advanced only to its authorized conclusion, regardless of malicious motives. It is not an abuse of process where a patient institutes a malpractice action against his physician, even without probable cause, but it is an abuse of process where the frivolous action was commenced for the sole purpose of forcing a settlement, even though courts favor settlements. But in the Texas case of Martin v. Trevino (supra) the physician plaintiff argued that the earlier malpractice case was instituted against him in order to "profit at the physician's expense" by at least coercing a settlement, but the court ruled that the complaint failed to allege an improper use of the citation. To the same effect is Brody v. Ruby (supra), where the Iowa Supreme Court reasoned that "settlement of actions is a positive goal of courts in order to avoid unnecessary and lengthy litigation." However, if the attorney knows that there is no basis for the claim of malpractice and institutes the action for the ulterior motive or purpose of obtaining even a "nuisance" settlement, then a finding of abuse of process is proper. (See 65 *Marquette Law Review* 93, 1981.) In the California case of Umansky v. Urguhart (84 Cal App3d, 368, 1978) the patient in a malpractice suit against his physician sought punitive damages, not withstanding a statutory prohibition against punitive damages in wrongful death cases. By stipulation of the parties an amended complaint which deleted the request for punitive damages was filed. The physician then filed a countersuit for abuse of process, asserting, inter alia, that the patient's sole reason for originally asking for punitive damages was the ulterior motive of embarrassing the physician and coercing him into settlement. But the California Court of Appeals affirmed the dismissal of the physician's suit, stating that, despite the current statutory bar to punitive damages, the law is not immutable and it is therefore reasonable for an attorney and his client to hope that they might change existing law!

In England in 1838 in Grainger v. Hill (132 Eng Rep 769) the defendant had the plaintiff arrested under civil process in order to compel plaintiff to surrender the register of a vessel without which plaintiff could not go to sea. The English court refused to permit its process to be misused for such ulterior purposes and held the defendant liable in damages. A century later, in the state of New Jersey in Ash v. Cohn (194 A 174, 1937), a judgment creditor, in order to avoid the trouble of having the sheriff seize the debtor's property and sell it to satisfy the judgment, had the debtor arrested on a warrant, and the judgment debtor promptly and directly paid the judgment. But the judgment debtor had a cause of action for abuse of process, even though the underlying suit had not been terminated in favor of the judgment creditor. Indeed, abuse of process differs from malicious prosecution (Chapter 4 herein) in that the gist of the tort of abuse of process is not in commencing an action or in causing process to issue without justification, but in misusing or perverting the process for an end or purpose for which the process was not designed (Abernethy v. Burns, 188 SE 97, NC, 1936).

3.2 PUNITIVE DAMAGES

Malice is not an element in abuse of process except on the issue of punitive damages (Saliem v. Glovsky, 172 A 4, Me, 1934); the improper end or improper purpose, as where a person prosecutes another in order to extort payment of a debt, is at the heart of the cause of action. The use of a subpoena to harass a person rather than for the proper purpose of obtaining testimony constitutes abuse of process (Illustration 3 of Section 682 of Restatement (Second) of Torts). In Rebore v. Pace, decided on December 5, 1985, by the New York Appellate Division, 2nd Dept., the plaintiffs commenced an action to recover damages for abuse of process in that plaintiffs were also served with a summons and complaint in a libel action against their attorney, who had represented plaintiffs on a pro bono basis in their defense of another libel action brought against them by the same defendants. As a result of the libel action against the attorney, the attorney was disqualified from acting as counsel to the plaintiffs on the grounds that "in light of his personal knowledge and involvement in the underlining (?) matter he would be clearly called as a witness and after consolidation of the two libel actions he would become a party defendant." Plaintiffs alleged that the second libel action against their attorney was "for the sole purpose of depriving them of the choice of counsel, thereby causing them to incur substantial legal fees." But the New York court ruled that the cause of action for abuse of process could not be maintained:

> The process complained of must involve an unlawful interference with one's person or property (Williams v. Williams 23 NY2d 592, 596). The only process issued in the action against Bartholomew J. Rebore was a summons and complaint, "the process necessary to obtain jurisdiction and begin the lawsuit. . . . there was no unlawful interference with plaintiffs' persons or property because the institution of a civil action by summons and complaint is not legally considered process capable of being abused" (Curiano v. Suozzi, 63 NY2d, 113, at 116). The disqualification of Mr. Rebore, which is essentially the detriment complained of, was obtained by defendants independent of the commencement of their action against Mr. Rebore. In addition to his status as a potential party defendant, he was also a material witness to the underlying events, which alone, supported his disqualification. Thus, as service of the summons and complaint was entirely unnecessary to the attainment of the harm complained of, the complaint was properly dismissed.

On the other hand, in Bull v. McCuskey (615 P2d 957, Nev, 1980) a physician had treated an eighty-six-year-old woman for orthopedic injuries sustained in an automobile accident. The woman was hospitalized for three months in one hospital, then transferred to another hospital. She was depressed, uncooperative, and uncommunicative, the Nevada court observed. While in the second hospital, bed sores developed on her hips and heels, and her nephew brought suit, charging the physician in the second hospital with medical malpractice. Before filing suit, the nephew's attorney did not examine or obtain hospital records, nor did he confer with a physician. He did not submit the complaint to a screening panel. Prior to trial, he offered to settle for $750. After a trial at which the attorney made several offensive comments about the physician, the jury returned a verdict in the physician's favor. The physician then countersued the attorney, claiming misuse of regularly issued process, or abuse of process. A jury awarded the physician $85,000, and the attorney appealed, but the highest Nevada court upheld the $85,000 award to the physician. The Nevada court said that compensatory damages in an action for abuse of process may include compensation for fears, anxiety, and emotional distress. The award of $35,000 compensatory damages was supported by the evidence, the court ruled; with respect to the punitive damages of $50,000, the jury could conclude that the suit was filed and the settlement offer made intentionally and with reckless disregard of the consequences.

The "process" itself must be compulsory in the sense that it compels performance or forebearance of certain specific conduct before its misuse can give rise to an action for abuse of process (Martin-Trigona v. Brooks & Holtzman, 551 F Supp 1378, NY, 1982). The use of a validly issued but erroneous or voidable process is not abuse of process (Laird v. Vogel, 334 So2d 650, Fla, 1976). In Pennsylvania as of 1980 a state statute (42 Pa Cons Stat Ann, Section 8351) delineated a tort of wrongful use of process in terms of liability for one who "acts in a grossly negligent manner"; a subsequent Pennsylvania decision (Schaffer v. Stewart, 473 A2d 1017, 1984) appears to construe the abuse of process as requiring malice which is generally not an element in the cause of action. A 1983 South Carolina decision, Johnson v. Painter (307 Se2d 860) also speaks of malicious misuse or perversion of process after its issuance for an end not lawfully warranted by it. For an attorney to be held liable for abuse of process the acts complained of must be his own acts or the acts of others that are "wholly instigated and carried on" by the attorney (Adelman v. Rosenbaum, 3A2d 15, Pa, 1938).

Wrongful civil process and abuse of process are frequently confused, for they both relate to the frivolous suit problem, but the former presupposes a meritless action initiated without foundation, while the latter punishes persons who commence a justifiable action for the purpose of attaining improper collateral objectives. Both remedies, however, seek to protect free access to judicial relief unfettered by frivolous lawsuits, frivolous answers, frivolous appeals, and frivolous subjectmatters. Wrongful civil process attacks frivolous litigation in particular, while abuse of process focuses upon misapplication of the judicial process.

3.3 WRONGFUL ATTACHMENT

Attachment is a prejudgment remedy which allows a creditor to secure payment of a judgment that may eventually be awarded; it is also a remedy for gaining jurisdiction over a non-resident with property or interests in the jurisdiction. Attachments permit a creditor who has filed a prima facie claim to have the debtor's assets seized and held until final adjudication, and it is this aspect of attachment that frequently lends itself to abuse, such as the attaching of exempt assets or more assets than are necessary to secure a claim. (See generally 30 *UCLA Law Review* 1218, 1983.) Abuse of process occurs when a wrongful act is committed, i.e., an act not justified in the regular course of the proceedings, as in White Lighting Co. v. Wolfson (438 P2d 345, Cal, 1968); there must be an ulterior or wrongful purpose for committing that wrongful act (Spellens v. Spellens, 317 P2d 613, Cal, 1957); and some injury must result from the wrongful act. Where the creditor seized the property of a party other than the debtor, as in Templeton Feed and Grain Co. v. Ralston Purina Co. (446 P2d 152, Cal, 1968) or where the creditor levied an excessive attachment, as in White Lighting Co. v. Wolfson (supra), abuse of process was clearly found. But in Pete v. Norberg (329 P2d 20, 1958) the California court disapproved of plaintiff's contention that an abuse of process occurred because the defendant creditor had garnished wages which were exempt as necessaries:

> There is no . . . evidence that defendant (attaching party) knew before the court's order of March 12 that plaintiff's claim of total exemption was valid. No further levies were made after that date. There is no showing that defendant acted other than in good faith in pursuing his admitted right of attachment or took any further steps after appellant's right to exemption was established. The findings negative the bad motive or ulterior purpose which is essential to the action where the process is regularly issued and employed.

On the other hand, in White Lighting Co. v. Wolfson (supra) the California court readily found abuse of process because the creditor with a claim for only $850 attached property alleged to be worth $20,000. And in Randone v. Appellate Department (488 P2d 13, 1971; cert den 407 US 454, 1972), a group of lawyers assigned their claims against the plaintiff for unpaid legal fees to a collection agency that sued plaintiff and attached plaintiff's checking account, although at the time plaintiff's sole source of income was unemployment insurance. The California Supreme Court recognized the extreme hardship and held that the debtors cannot be deprived of "necessary" assets without a full judicial hearing on the validity of the underlying claim at trial. Furthermore, Section 487.020 of the California Civil Procedure Code stated that all property "necessary for the support of an individual . . . or family" is exempt from attachment.

3.4 CRIMINAL ASPECTS

Abuse of process, being an intentional misuse of a legitimate court process for some ulterior or collateral purpose, is truly a form of extortion and has certain criminal aspects. Abuse of process in the criminal field is illustrated by State ex rel Richardson v. Edgeworth (214 So2d 579, 1968), where the Mississippi Supreme Court found the defendant justices of the peace liable for using criminal processes of the court solely for the collection of civil debts, to wit:

> (1) permitting people to sign criminal affidavits without advising them of the criminal nature of the documents; (2) failing to require affiants to appear before the justice of the peace for sworn statements; (3) permitting criminal affidavits to be signed in blank; (4) charging excessive mileage; (5) soliciting collection of accounts, through their deputy sheriffs and constables; and (6) using the criminal processes for the collection of civil debts alone.

The prisoner Richardson, as the direct result of these "intentional torts-the abuse of process," committed suicide, and the defendants were held liable for his death.

It is the ulterior motive of the person utilizing the process of the court that is paramount; ulterior motive may be shown by the collateral advantage directly demanded by the defendant resulting in the abuse of process (Trachina v. Arcinas, 178 P2d 65, Cal, 1947). Ulterior motive may be inferred from the manner in which the process was carried out, as where a lawyer filed an unfounded and uninvestigated medical malpractice claim and then demanded settlement for a small amount of money; at the trial he produced no medical expert testimony but continued his method of attempting to extort a nuisance settlement (Bull v. McCuskey, supra). An ulterior motive plus an act to accomplish that motive after process has been issued is all that is required. Courts have held that receipt of judgments against a person who owed no money (Little v. Sowers, 204 P2d 605, Kan, 1949) or the use of force in the service of a summons and complaint was a perversion of legal process (Remes v. Duby, 244 NW2d 440, Mich, 1976). Comment a to Section 682 of Restatement (Second) of Torts provides a suitable example of abuse of process:

> A, an attorney to whom C has entrusted the collection of a debt owed by B, assigns C's claim to D, who resides some distance from B. In accordance with A's instructions, D brings an action as assignee and causes a subpoena to issue at a time when it is extremely inconvenient for B to appear, A's purpose being to force B to pay the claim rather than to undergo the inconvenience of appearance. B not appearing, A causes a bench warrant to issue for his arrest under which B is fined and execution against his body is ordered. Before this order is carried out, B brings his action against A. A is subject to liability to B for abuse of process.

3.5 LAWYERS AND ABUSE OF PROCESS

In California in 1974 the defendant attorney together with nine other lawyers filed a complaint with the State Bar Association accusing lawyer Younger of "ambulance chasing." The client Jenkins in a separate suit accused Younger of intentional infliction of mental injuries and emotional distress growing out of Younger's allegedly fraudulent solicitation of the personal injury claim of Jenkins; Jenkins also contended that Younger had wrongfully interfered with the settlement negotiations that Jenkins herself had been conducting with an insurance company. Defendant Younger cross-claimed against all the plaintiffs, alleging abuse of process in that the ten attorneys had allegedly persuaded Jenkins to sue him. The trial court dismissed Younger's cross-claim, and the California Court of Appeals in Younger v. Solomon (38 Cal App3d 289) opined:

The term "process" as used in the tort of Abuse of Process has been broadly interpreted to encompass the entire range of procedures incident to litigation. Written interrogatories which are specifically authorized by Code of Civil Procedure, Section 2030, and in this case enforced with sanctions by the trial court, clearly come within the range of procedures incident to litigation; thus, the use of the interrogatory constituted the use of "process."

Was there an "abuse" of the process? The gist of the tort is the misuse of the power of the court: It is an act done under the authority of the court for the purpose of perpetrating an injustice, i.e., a perversion of the judicial process to the accomplishment of an improper purpose. Some definite act or threat not authorized by the process or aimed at an objective not legitimate in the use of the process is required. And, generally, an action lies only where the process is used to obtain an unjustifiable collateral advantage. For this reason, mere vexation or harassment are not recognized as objectives sufficient to give rise to the tort.

But the appellate court reversed the trial court upon finding abuse of process, to wit:

[The] disclosure and publication of the fact that a complaint against appellant for professional misconduct had been filed with the State Bar by ten Kern County attorneys. It may be inferred that this was done to damage appellant's reputation as a lawyer and thereby unfairly eliminate or impede his activities as a competitor in the practice of law. Such an inference is reasonable because, as an attorney, respondent could be expected to appreciate the serious impact which the publication of the charges of professional misconduct would have on appellant's relationship with clients, judges and other attorneys in Kern County.

In the past few years, according to the *National Law Journal* (November 11, 1985, at p. 1), "In ever-growing numbers, State and federal judges are hitting lawyers with costly economic sanctions for abuse of process in civil litigation—

and those lawyers include some from the nation's most prestigious firms. Bolstered by recent changes in the rules of civil procedure, some judges have imposed fines in the six-figure range, while others have sent unflattering opinions about the attorneys' conduct to be published.'' One example is in Westmoreland v. CBS, Inc. (770 F2d 1168, DC Cir, 1985), where the District of Columbia Court of Appeals instructed the lower court to award attorney fees to opposing lawyers for wrongfully conducting a videotaped deposition without first obtaining a stipulation or court order permitting it. In SMF Corp. v. Sundstrand Corp. (102 FRD 555, 1985) the federal district court took a dim view of a motion for partial summary judgment in a contract dispute that was ''plainly brimming with disputed issues of material fact.'' Similarly, in Wells v. Oppenheimer (101 FRD 358, 1984) a federal district court in New York was angered by a motion for summary judgment when ''questions of fact were obvious and . . . the motion was a futile one.'' It should be noted that Rule 11 of the Federal Rules of Civil Procedure with respect to signing motions, pleadings, and other legal papers, effective August 1, 1983, obliges lawyers to make a ''reasonable inquiry'' into the factual and legal basis of any paper filed in court. The attorney's signature is a personal certification that the document is ''well grounded in fact and is warranted by existing law or a good faith argument for the extension, modification, or reversal of existing law, and . . . not interposed for any improper purpose, such as to harass or to cause unnecessary delay or needless increase in the cost of litigation.''

Another new FRCP rule, 26 (g), requires since 1983 that a lawyer's signature of a discovery request or response be subject to the same standards of certification. Rule 16 (f) authorizes sanctions against any lawyer or party who is unprepared to participate in pre-trial conferences or who fails to participate in good faith. The Third U.S. Court of Appeals in Eash v. Riggins Trucking, Inc. (757 F2d 557, 1985) summarized:

> The dramatic rise in litigation in the last decade has led trial judges to conclude that indulgent toleration of the lawyer's misconduct is simply a luxury the federal court system can no longer afford.

It should be observed that one of the hazards of practicing law for lawyers is the claim of a non-client or a person not in the attorney-client relationship. But the general rule appears to exempt the attorney from liability to such third persons who might even be harmed as a result of his lawful professional acts or omissions for the benefit of his client. See 30 *South Carolina Law Review* 203 (1979).

The sole caveat has been stated by the Court of Appeals for the District of Columbia in Morowitz v. Marvel (423 A2d 196, 1980), which opined:

> It is axiomatic that the American system of jurisprudence favors free access to the courts as a medium of dispute settlement. It is the announced policy of this jurisdiction to

allow unfettered access to our courts. In an effort to avoid infringing upon the right of the public to utilize our courts, we are cautious not to adopt rules which will have a chilling and inhibitory effect on would-be litigants of justiciable issues.

An interesting variation on the action of malicious prosecution occurred in Cerbone v. Conway, decided by the Second U.S. Court of Appeals in early 1986. Here the plaintiff sued a local car dealership and its attorney (also the local village judge) for malicious prosecution after the defendants had her arrested and prosecuted when she stopped payment on a check for car repairs that the dealership allegedly performed badly. Simultaneously plaintiff instituted an action in the federal courts for violation of her civil rights, and the defendants argued that the federal civil rights action must fall where a state remedy is available. But the court ruled that, since the facts which gave rise to the claim spelled out a deprivation of her liberty (not merely a deprivation of property), she was entitled to maintain both the state and the federal causes of action against the defendants. The U.S. Supreme Court agreed to hear the case in late 1986.

4

Malicious Prosecution

4.1 THE NATURE OF THE CAUSE OF ACTION

The interest in freedom from unjustifiable or frivolous litigation is protected also by the action for malicious prosecution, which historically was derived from the now generally defunct torts of barratry, champerty, and maintenance that originated in the criminal field. (See Norton v. Hines, 49 Cal App3d 917, 1975.) The obsolete action for barratry depended upon statute and was rarely brought because of the difficulty of proof that a person with evil intent wickedly and willfully incited and stirred up a lawsuit or civil quarrel with a view toward promoting strife and contention. What gave the action for malicious prosecution a boost was the enactment by the English Parliament in the year 1269 of the Statute of Marlbridge (52 Hen III), which provided for a summary proceeding and for the winning defendant to recover in the same action his costs and attorney's fee once he proved damages, although the requirement of ''damages'' was later eliminated by the Act of 23 Henry VIII, chapter 15.

The tort of malicious prosecution was adopted in the United States from its English antecedents requiring a plaintiff to plead and prove malice, lack of probable cause, favorable termination, and a ''special injury'' beyond that normally incurred in defending a lawsuit (Harter v. Lewis Stores, Inc., 240 SW2d 86, Ky, 1961). The English requirement of ''special injury'' connoted deprivation of liberty or property in contrast to mere humiliation, embarrassment, and emotional anguish (Greer v. State Farm Fire & Casualty Co., 227 SE2d 881, Ga, 1976). But a bare majority of states have eliminated the ''special injury'' requirement, pointing out that malicious prosecution is not a secondary remedy nor is it unaccompanied by an internal sanction system in the United

States (Cisson v. Pickens Savings and Loan Assn., 186 SE2d 822, SC, 1972). Section 674 of Restatement (Second) of Torts follows the bare majority rule requiring no "special damages," and limits damages recoverable to attorneys' fees, costs, and other similar damages, in contrast to the minority of English rule requiring proof of "special injury," which sanctions recovery of actual, unlimited damages (Bickel v. Mackie, 477 F Supp 1376, Iowa, 1976). "Special injury" might encompass wrongful arrest of the person, seizure of his property, or an injury different than the normal incidents of defending a lawsuit. Obviously, such items as expenses of litigation or damage to reputation or loss of time to defend the suit do not constitute "special injury" (Balthazar v. Dowling, 382 NE2d 1257, Ill, 1978). For a comprehensive listing of states in 1977 that had or had not the "special injury" requisite, see O'Toole v. Franklin, 569 P2d 561, Ore, 1977.

A malicious prosecution action may be brought against the client as well as against the client's attorney (Berlin v. Nathan, 381 NE2d 1367, Ill, 1978). While the attorney generally owes no duty of care to his client's adversary (and generally an attorney will be liable only to his own client for negligence, not to third parties, as illustrated by Nelson v. Miller, 607 P2d 438, Kan, 1980), nevertheless the attorney cannot totally ignore the adversary client's rights when the attorney institutes the suit.

The cause of action for malicious prosecution embraces the following elements: (1) prior legal proceedings which were commenced or were continued by the present defendant against the present plaintiff, i.e., institution or continuance of prior proceeding, delineated at §4.2 herein; (2) a bona fide termination of the prior legal proceeding in favor of the present plaintiff, i.e., termination of prior proceeding in favor of present plaintiff, described at §4.3 herein; (3) absence of probable cause in present defendant's institution of the prior legal proceeding, i.e., absence of probable cause, set forth at §4.4 herein; (4) improper purpose or malice on the part of the present defendant in instituting the prior legal proceeding, i.e., malice in instituting or continuing proceeding, described at §4.5 herein; and (5) damages resulting to the present plaintiff, i.e., damages resulting from proceeding, delineated at §4.6 herein. Some of the defenses to malicious prosecution are set forth in §4.7 herein, and in §4.8 are described the privileged complaints that can be made to bar associations against attorneys.

At the outset it should be noted that malicious prosecution does not pertain to an injury to the person, but does describe an injury to reputation, even though damages for emotional distress, inter alia, have been awarded today in the United States (Carruth v. Superior Court, 80 Cal App3d 215, 1978).

It should also be observed that it is the attorney who bears the brunt of malicious prosecution actions, and the aggrieved person bases this suit upon some breach of duty allegedly owed to him by the attorney. But courts are more interested in minimizing this duty of attorneys to third parties as indicated above, in order to avoid the appearance of a conflict of interest that could result from recognition of an attorney's duty of care to both his client and to his client's adversary (Norton v. Hines, 49 Cal App3d 917, 1975). Indeed, in the final analysis, the courts must balance this recognition against the rights of wrongfully sued defendants to be compensated.

4.2 INSTITUTION OR CONTINUANCE OF PRIOR PROCEEDING

The initial ingredient in the cause of action for malicious prosecution is that there must have been a prior legal proceeding, civil or criminal or even administrative, which had been commenced or continued by the present defendant against the present plaintiff. The "prior proceeding" concept was delineated at length by the District of Columbia Court of Appeals in Melvin v. Pence (130 F2d 423, 1942), where plaintiff, a duly licensed private detective, instituted an action for malicious prosecution against the licensing authorities who had refused to renew his license because he allegedly impersonated a police officer; at a subsequent administrative hearing, the plaintiff's license was renewed. At the outset of the opinion, the court observed that the "proceedings were administrative, not judicial in character"; but the court asserted:

> Access to the courts and other tribunals, however, should not be abused. The freedom to use their processes is not absolute. When malice motivates a groundless claim and results in special injury beyond what assertion of rights ordinarily entails, remedy is afforded. The right to litigate is not the right to become a nuisance. When the proceeding has no relation to protection of any right of the suitor or any public right which he reasonably may have a hand in vindicating, the reason for his protection fails and he must respond.
>
> We agree with plaintiff that these principles are clearly applicable to administrative proceedings. Much of the jurisdiction formerly residing in the courts has been transferred to administrative tribunals, and much new jurisdiction involving private rights and penal consequences has been vested in them. In a broad sense their creation involves the emergence of a new system of courts not less significant than the evolution of chancery. The same harmful consequences may flow from the groundless and malicious institution of proceedings in them as does from judicial proceedings similarly begun. When one's livelihood depends upon a public license, it makes little difference to him whether it is taken away by a court or by an administrative body or official. Nor should his right to redress the injury depend upon the technical form of the proceeding by which it is inflicted. The administrative process is also a legal process, and its abuse in the same way with the same injury should receive the same penalty.
>
> We agree, therefore, with the Court of Appeals for the Fourth Circuit that the reason of the rule applies to administrative, as it does to judicial proceedings, and therefore that the rule itself also should apply to them.

On the other hand, it is stated in Section 654 of Restatement (Second) of Torts that any proceeding of a criminal character will support an action for malicious prosecution, although it must be a judicial proceeding and not a mere investigation by the district attorney (Losi v. Natalicchio, 112 NYS2d 706, 1952). However, it is sufficient that a warrant had been issued for the present plaintiff's arrest, although the warrant was never served (Halberstadt v. New York Life Insurance Co., 86 NE 801, NY, 1909); it is the commencement of the prior legal proceeding that is paramount. Even an unsuccessful cross-action, cross-claim, or counterclaim can be the basis of the malicious prosecution suit (Wilson v. Brooks, 369 So2d 1221, Ala, 1979); in fact, any procedural device which seeks affirmative relief is a basis for malicious prosecution when the device is used for strategic purposes such as the harassment of an adversary, the frustration or delay in prosecuting the principal action, or for the purpose of coercing a disadvantageous settlement (Bertero v. National General Corp., 529 P2d 608, Cal, 1975).

The present defendant must have instituted or continued the legal proceeding, as illustrated by Boyd v. Hodson (72 NE2d 46, Ind app, 1947), where the defendants made statements to official investigators who subsequently brought about the prosecution of the present plaintiff for sending lewd and lascivious letters through the mail. The Indiana appellate court opined that, since such statements by the defendants played a material role in bringing about the prosecution of the present plaintiff, the requirement that defendants must have instituted or caused it to be instituted was satisfied. Defendants must indeed have taken an active part in instigating and encouraging the prosecution (Schleicher v. Western State Bank, 314 NW2d 293, ND, 1982). A present defendant can be liable for continuing, active participation after learning of exculpatory facts even though he could not be liable for instituting the prosecution in the first place (Lampos v. Bazar, Inc., 527 P2d 976, Ore, 1974). But merely furnishing information to a prosecutor for his investigation is not generally actionable (Vehrs v. Piquette, 684 P2d 476, Mont, 1984). The prosecutor himself is absolutely immune from suits for malicious prosecution even if he is shown to have acted in bad faith; this immunity is vital to the performance of the duties of the prosecutor as long as he is acting within the general scope of his official duties. Even an administrative judge is accorded the same immunity, as shown in Butz v. Economou (438 US 478, 1978).

In analyzing the essence of malicious prosecution, it should be observed that litigation is the accepted social means for resolving disputes that cannot otherwise be settled and that prosecution does encourage honest citizens to bring criminals or tortfeasors to justice. Consequently, the law gives the accuser a large degree of freedom to make mistakes of fact and commit errors of judgment without being subjected to liability. But no one is permitted to subject another person to prosecution for an improper purpose and without an honest belief that the accused may be found guilty or liable for the wrong perpetrated. Freedom from unjustifiable or frivolous litigation must be balanced against the social interest in supporting resort to law and utilization of legal institutions. A pathologist who erroneously reported that the present plaintiff's wife had died of a blow to the skull was held not liable in a malicious prosecution action brought by the husband in Bromund v. Holt (129 NW2d 149, Wis, 1964) because the greater ends of justice demanded non-liability on the part of the responding pathologist.

It should be noted that suits against attorneys under theories of negligence (Bikel v. Mackie, supra), prima facie tort (Drago v. Buonagurio, 386 NE2d 821, NY, 1978), and even violation of an attorney's code of professional ethics (see §8.6 herein) have proved to be generally unacceptable, for courts are loathe to create an unduly broad duty of care for an attorney which might impair the earnest prosecution or defense of the claim. However, an early Kansas decision, Maechtlen v. Clapp (250 P 303, Kan, 1926), had imposed a rigorous standard, to wit:

> An attorney who knowingly permits a client to make him an instrument of prosecuting a party against whom the client had no ground of complaint or cause of action, or was bringing the action through animosity or some malicious motive is accountable to the party wronged as much as if the suit was prompted by his own malice. . . .

4.3 TERMINATION OF PRIOR PROCEEDING IN FAVOR OF PRESENT PLAINTIFF

A second requisite of the cause of action for malicious prosecution is that the prior legal proceeding instituted or continued by the present defendant was terminated and resulted in favor of the present plaintiff (Foster v. Turner, 319 So2d 233, Miss, 1975). Where the prior action was terminated by abandonment or by failure to prosecute, the burden of proof shifts dramatically to the present plaintiff, who must explain the reasons; Section 665 of Restatement (Second) of Torts appears to preclude a finding of favorable termination of the prior legal proceeding where the prior action is abandoned due to discovery of facts exculpating the present plaintiff. In Lumpkin v. Friedman (131 Cal App3d 450, 1982) a dismissal arising from a failure to comply with a discovery requirement was deemed a favorable termination tantamount to a failure to prosecute. And in Zeavin v. Lee (136 Cal App3d 766, 1982) the rule was not applied to an attorney when the dismissal resulted from the client's unilateral abandonment of the action. Prevailing on only one or some of the theories or causes of action is not a favorable termination, according to the Missouri court in Boyer v. Carondelet Savings & Loan Assn. (633 SW2d 98, 1982). A "plea bargain" in which the present plaintiff pleaded guilty to some other offense did not meet the "favorable disposition" requirement set forth in Section 660 (a) of Restatement (Second) of Torts.

The requisite of favorable termination of the prior legal proceeding also reflects the merits and the maturity of the prior legal proceeding (Lackner v. LaCroix, 602 P2d 393, Cal, 1979). But where charges are withdrawn or the criminal prosecution is terminated at the instigation of the accused himself or by reason of a compromise into which he has voluntarily entered, there is no sufficient ''termination'' in favor of the present plaintiff (Mondrow v. Selwyn, 412 A2d 447, NJ, 1980). The reasoning is that this conduct is an admission of ''probable cause'' (see §4.4 herein) and merely postpones the eventual decision that may or may not be favorable to the present plaintiff. In Leonard v. George (178 F2d 312, 4th Cir, 1949) the Fourth U.S. Court of Appeals faced a situation of a plaintiff who had been the manager of defendants' farm upon which turkeys were being raised. Defendants' superintendent caused a warrant to be issued charging plaintiff with fraudulent breach of trust in the sale of certain turkeys. Plaintiff was arrested, jailed, and then released after paying $415 to the superintendent to have the criminal prosecution dismissed. The court took the view that plaintiff had compromised and settled the case, and therefore the prior legal proceeding had not been ''favorably terminated'' so as to permit plaintiff to recover in this malicious prosecution action:

> Notwithstanding the protests and declarations of plaintiff made at the time, we think that he is unquestionably precluded by the settlement from suing for malicious prosecution with respect to the case thus disposed of. He thoroughly understood what he was doing and there is nothing to indicate that he was coerced as the result of imprisonment or duress of any sort. On the contrary, plaintiff had been released on bail at the time. The case seems to be clearly one for the application of the rule stated in A.L.I. Restatement of Torts, vol. 3, p. 400, as follows: ''c. Compromise. Although the accused by his acceptance of a compromise does not admit his guilt, the fact of compromise indicates that the question of his guilt or innocence is left open. Having bought peace the accused may not thereafter assert that the proceedings have terminated in his favor.'' The reason for the rule was well stated by Lord Tenterden in the old case of Wilkinson v. Howel, Moody & M. 495, where he said, ''I think this mode of termination does not furnish any evidence that the action was without probable cause. If this should be allowed, the defendant would be deceived by the consent, as, without that, he would certainly have gone on with the action, and might have shown a foundation for it. I have no doubt about it.''

Indeed, ''compromise'' has been made synonymous with ''non-favorable termination'' (Tucker v. Duncan, 499 F2d 963, 4th Cir, 1974). But in Hammond Lead Products Co. v. American Cyanamid Co. (570 F2d 688, 7th Cir, 1977) the court authorized proof of defendant's guilt or innocence in the very malicious prosecution action, rather than simply considering whether the prior legal proceeding satisfied the requisite of a favorable termination.

The requisite of favorable termination of the prior proceeding is attested to by a recognition that concurrent actions might result in deprivation of effective counsel for the present plaintiff as defendant in the original action, i.e., should the second action for malicious prosecution be allowed to commence at the same time or before the termination of the prior proceeding. Also of concern is the possibility that juries or courts in two separate actions might render inconsistent verdicts or judgments (Parrott v. Plowden Motor Co., 143 SE2d

607, SC, 1965). Likewise, the action for malicious prosecution cannot be initiated by way of cross-complaint or counterclaim in the original proceeding (Babb v. Superior Court, 479 P2d 379, Cal, 1971). In Minasian v. Sapse (80 Cal App3d 823, 1978) an attorney brought a malicious prosecution action against a former client who allegedly had filed a groundless cross-complaint and counterclaim in an action for recovery of attorney's fees. The California appellate court ruled that dismissal of defendant's cross-complaint and counterclaim for failure to prosecute was a favorable termination of the proceedings and therefore the malicious prosecution action was in order. But where the dismissal is construed to be part of a settlement agreement, as shown by the Alabama court in Wilson v. Brooks (369 So2d 1221, 1979), the favorable termination prerequisite was deemed not to be satisfied for purposes of the malicious prosecution action.

4.4 ABSENCE OF PROBABLE CAUSE

For the present plaintiff to succeed in his malicious prosecution action he must show that the present defendant lacked "probable cause" in instituting the prior legal proceedings. In general, the present defendant will be held to have had "probable cause" if he correctly or reasonably believed that the present plaintiff had committed certain acts, and that these acts constituted a tort or a crime, according to Section 662 of Restatement (Second) of Torts. One example is found in the 1962 English decision of Glinki v. McIver (A.C. 726), decided by the House of Lords; here plaintiff sued police on the ground that they unsuccessfully, out of ill-will, prosecuted him for conspiracy. Lord Radcliffe opined:

> The action for malicious prosecution is by now a well-trodden path. I take it to be settled law that if the defendant can be shown to have initiated the prosecution without himself holding an honest belief in the truth of the charge (I must, of course, refine on this phrase later) he cannot be said to have acted upon reasonable and probable cause. The connection between the two ideas is not very close at first sight, for one would suppose that there might well exist reasonable and probable cause in the objective sense, what one might call a good case, irrespective of the state of the prosecutor's own mind or his personal attitude towards the validity of the case. The answer is, I think, that the ultimate question is not so much whether there is reasonable or probable cause in fact as whether the prosecutor, in launching his charge, was motivated by what presented itself to him as a reasonable and probable cause. Hence, if he did not believe that there was one, he must have been in the wrong.

The House of Lords accordingly found that the police were not liable as they had "probable cause" in prosecuting the present plaintiff.

In Carroll v. Kalar (112 Ariz 595, 545 P2d 411) the Arizona Supreme Court in 1976 held that the present plaintiff had not proven his case for malicious prosecution because the present defendant and his attorney had "probable cause" for bringing the action against the defendant physician, at least based upon the advice obtained from a medical expert to the effect that the plaintiff physician's treatment was below the standard of care in the community. It seems that plaintiff physician here had allegedly performed an operation based upon x-rays that were five or six years old.

It is clear that malicious prosecution is an action that runs counter to those policies in the law that seek the end to litigation, for the action does give the winning, prior defendant a second chance to even up matters. The unpopularity of the malicious prosecution action to the judiciary has prompted restrictions such as the requisite absence of "probable cause." This dichotomy was delineated at length by Judge Edgerton of the U.S. Court of Appeals for the District of Columbia in Soffos v. Eaton (152 F2d 682, 1945) as follows:

> The law tries to avoid both too much discouragement and too much encouragement of litigation. Some sort of balance has to be struck between the social interests in preventing unconscionable suits and in permitting honest assertion of supposed rights. These interests conflict because a suit which its author thinks honest may look unconscionable to a jury. Probably some suits which ought to be brought would not be brought if the inevitable risk of losing a suit always carried with it the further risk of having to defend a charge that it was brought maliciously and without probable cause.

Indeed, it has been argued that courts do not and should not permit parties to misuse the judiciary, especially where one party sues another without "probable cause," as set forth in Norton v. Hines (49 Cal App3d 917). In a 1975 trial the present plaintiff Norton was alleged to have induced the breach of a contract; but the case was dismissed when the attorney for the present defendant conceded that there was no evidence to support the complaint. Then Norton brought this action against plaintiff's attorney for malicious prosecution. Although the California Court of Appeals agreed that an attorney could be held liable when an attorney brings a suit based upon a claim that a reasonable attorney would not regard as tenable and where that attorney unreasonably neglected to investigate the facts and the law, the court nevertheless decided that here the attorney should *not* be held liable. Actually, the case was dismissed because Norton declined to spend additional monies to amend his pleadings to conform to the necessary statutory pleadings in an action for malicious prosecution. It is apparent that a different standard was applied to the attorney, for courts frequently scrutinize the attorney's ethical and professional obligations to his client (Wong v. Taylor, 422 NE2d 1279, Ind, 1981). Compliance by an attorney with these obligations is said to comport with the requirement of "probable cause." A standard based upon an adversary's rights is vague and unreliable and is likely to distract an attorney from aggressively pursuing his client's cause. An attorney cannot be held to guarantee the success or the quality of his client's cause; frequently the attorney must consciously prosecute or defend cases which cannot become successful (Petrou v. Hale, 260 SE2d 130,

NC, 1979). Ethical obligations basic to the profession dictate that an attorney must not reject a cause because of its difficulty or even impossibility of success (Berlin v. Nathan, 381 NE2d 1367, Ill, 1978). Courts have therefore cautioned against criticizing or penalizing an attorney for pursuing a case which appears to have little chance or even no chance of winning, since these very actions often account for changes in the law (Junot v. Lee, 372 So2d 707, La, 1979). More than 150 years ago the Massachusetts Supreme Judicial Court in Bicknell v. Dorion (33 Mass 478, 1835) concluded that a malicious prosecution action against the attorney could not succeed unless the present plaintiff could prove that the attorney and his client knew at the outset that the action was groundless and lacked "probable cause," and also that both the attorney and his client were motivated by a "sinister" purpose. "Probable cause" requires no more than that there be a reasonable basis for the attorney to believe that the client has a tenable, justifiable, and non-frivolous claim (Fee, Parker & Lloyd v. Sullivan, 379 So2d 412, Fla, 1980). But an attorney is not immune from liability merely because he has acted on behalf of a client (Woycznski v. Wolf, 464 NE2d 612, Ohio, 1983). The Michigan Supreme Court in Friedman v. Dozoroc (312 NW2d 585, 1981) emphasized that an attorney's ethical obligations to his client required loyalty, tenacity, and single-mindedness of purpose; the attorney needs no more than a reasonable basis for believing that the claim might be valid, as delineated in Section 675 of Restatement (Second) of Torts.

In Weaver v. Superior Court (95 Cal App3d 166, 1979) the California court stated that as long as an attorney does not prosecute a claim which a reasonable attorney would not regard as tenable, or unreasonably neglect to investigate the facts and the law in making an investigation and determination to proceed, the opposing party has no right to assert malicious prosecution against the attorney. And in Moiel v. Sandlin (571 SW2d 567, Tex, 1978) the Texas court opined:

> An attorney may generally rely in good faith upon the facts his client relates. Unless lack of probable cause for a claim is obvious from the facts disclosed by the client or otherwise brought to the attorney's attention, he may assume the facts so disclosed are substantially correct.

It would appear from these two cases that some courts will bend over backwards to protect the attorney from malicious prosecution even where the attorney has been remiss in his duty and responsibility as an officer of the court. The vindictive physician lost the malicious prosecution action in Fee, Parker & Lloyd v. Sullivan (supra) as the Florida District Court of Appeals protected the attorney. Here the original malpractice action alleged that the physician performed an unsuccessful closed reduction of a fracture of the patient's forearm, necessitating insertion of a rod into the forearm, which act subsequently required further surgery when the inserted rod turned out to be too long. After favorable determination of the malpractice action, the winning physician brought the malicious prosecution suit against the patient and his attorney, and the jury returned a verdict in favor of the physician in the sum of $175,000 (which the court reduced to $75,000). But the appellate court reversed, holding that the malpractice case established probable cause, not malpractice, and that all that was required was probable cause.

"Probable cause" is judged by appearances to the present defendant at the time that he initiated prosecution or sued the present plaintiff, not at the time when the facts were discovered subsequently (Oros v. City and County of Honolulu, 534 P2d 489, Haw, 1975). Where the present defendant was mistaken either as to the facts or as to the law, "probable cause" may still be indicated if his mistakes are "reasonable" under the circumstances. In Gustafson v. Payless Drug Stores Northwest, Inc. (525 P2d 118, Ore, 1974) the Oregon Supreme Court found an absence of "probable cause" in the present defendant charging a patron with the criminal charge of shoplifting. Quoting from its earlier decision in Varner v. Hoffer (515 P2d 920, 1973), the court again approved Section 662 of Restatement (Second) of Torts "as a correct statement of when probable cause exists." The Restatement provides:

> One who initiates criminal proceedings against another has probable cause for so doing if he
>
> (a) reasonably believes that the person accused has acted or failed to act in a particular manner, and
>
> (b)
> (i) correctly believes that such acts or omissions constitute at common law or under an existing statute the offense charged against the accused, or
> (ii) mistakenly so believes in reliance on the advice of counsel under the conditions statedin §666.

The court opined that "for the defendant to have probable cause, it must have both a reasonable belief in the guilt of the accused as well as a subjective belief," as determined by the court, not by the jury. Thereupon, the court concluded that plaintiff had proved lack of "probable cause": "Suspicion is not enough, but belief beyond a reasonable doubt is not necessary":

> After the plaintiff picked up the cigarettes she never concealed or attempted to conceal them. Plaintiff tendered payment to an employee at a checkstand. Plaintiff had an almost constant conversation with her mother-in-law as she walked through various parts of the store. Plaintiff waited immediately outside the store for five minutes engaging in further conversation. Mrs. Yaw was aware of this conduct.
>
> We admit that a subtle shoplifter could dispel suspicion by offering to pay at a checkstand where she knew her offer would not be accepted and by walking around a store carrying the merchandise she intended to steal in plain view. We are of the opinion, however, that the odds that a person so conducting herself is a shoplifter are so slight that this conduct, plus the other circumstances here present, does not amount to probable cause.

The strong dissent of Justice Holman pointed out that the above facts, as found by the majority,

> are relevant to whether plaintiff forgot to pay for the cigarettes, but they are absolutely irrelevant to whether the detective had probable cause to prosecute plaintiff for shoplifting and give an unwarranted cast favorable to the majority's conclusion which is not merited. We have previously held that the removal of merchandise from a store without paying for it is usually a basis for probable cause. Delp v. Zapp's Drug and Variety Stores, 238 Or. 538, 395 P2d 137, (1964). I would apply this rule under the circumstances here. Malicious prosecution cases are not favorites of the law because law enforcement depends in large part upon the complaints of citizens. It is well known that shoplifting is a national problem which causes businesses and, thus, customers loss of serious sums of money. The majority would make it impractical in most instances for security personnel to safely arrest and prosecute anyone for shoplifting. The policy to which the majority subscribes requires the store owner to walk too fine a line to be practical. I would rule that defendant had probable cause.

If the present defendant had in fact charged the present plaintiff with the criminal charge of shoplifting *upon the advice and counsel of its legal department,* it would appear that the dissenting opinion would be correct. In general, "probable cause" is established where the prosecution was instituted upon the advice of counsel (Reid v. True, 302 SW2d 846, Ky, 1957). The advice of counsel properly addresses the issue of "probable cause" because it bears upon the present defendant's reasonable belief that there was legal justification for the criminal or tortious proceeding, even though there were mistakes of fact. The counsel imparting the legal advice must be competent, duly admitted to practice law within the state, or apparently qualified to offer a trustworthy legal opinion (Truman v. Fidelity & Casualty Co., 123 SE2d 59, WVa, 1961).

Above all, courts in deciding issues of "probable cause" look toward the "reasonable man" under the circumstances, to wit: a reasonable man under the circumstances would or would not initiate or continue the proceedings against the present plaintiff. While it is the prerogative of the jury to respond to issues of fact and the court to respond to issues of law, most of the occurrences are in reality a mixture of law and fact, and therefore the determinations will be made differently in different jurisdictions. The state of Ohio, for example, permits the jury to respond to "probable cause" issues if more than one conclusion can be drawn as to the reasonableness of the present defendant's conduct (Edginton v. Glassmeyer, 168 NE2d 425, 1959).

4.5 MALICE IN INSTITUTING OR CONTINUING PROCEEDING

Equally important to the cause of action for malicious prosecution is the necessary element of "malice," and the present plaintiff has the burden of proof that the present defendant instituted the prior legal proceeding maliciously or for an improper purpose. Proof of absence of ''probable cause'' or evidence that the prior legal proceeding had been abandoned has supported an inference that the present defendant acted with malice. (The Oregon Supreme Court in Alvarez v. Retail Credit Assn., 381 P2d 499, 1963, took a contrary view.) The Arizona decision in Bradshaw v. State Farm Mutual Automobile Insurance Co., decided February 12, 1985, demonstrates how expensive a finding of ''malice'' can be in an action for malicious prosecution. Here a deputy sheriff was seriously injured when defendant's policyholder pulled out from a stop sign into the path of sheriff's patrol car; the insured was killed in the accident. Nine months after the accident the deputy sheriff offered to settle with the insurer for $100,000, the upper limits of the decedent's insurance policy, but the defendant carrier rejected the offer, appraising settlement between $65,000 and $75,000. Rather than continue to negotiate for settlement, the present defendant-insurer filed a wrongful death action against the deputy sheriff, although the carrier never made an attempt to prosecute the suit on behalf of the decedent. About a year and a half later, just before trial of the wrongful death action, the carrier offered to settle for $60,000, which amount the deputy sheriff accepted in exchange for dismissal of the wrongful death action. Thereupon, the deputy sheriff sued the carrier for abuse of process and for malicious malpractice. The trial judge granted the carrier a directed verdict as to the abuse of process claim, but allowed the jury to decide the claim for malicious prosecution, and the jury award was $40,000 for compensatory, mental distress and $2 million for punitive damages. (The court ordered a remittitur of $1,040,000.) The thrust of the decision was a tort of ''malicious defense,'' a common practice of some carriers whose only purpose is to harass the plaintiff to delay litigation, and to force unfair settlement, all of which efforts by the insurance carrier here ''boomeranged'' to its detriment by the deputy sheriff's successful action for malicious prosecution. See 35 *Hastings Law Journal* 891 (July 1984).

''Malice'' is shown, for example, when a lawyer acts for a purpose other than to secure a proper adjudication of his client's claim (Myers v. Cohen, 687 P2d 6, Haw, 1984). If a person is found to have acted chiefly to give vent to motives of ill-will and hatred, ''malice'' can be established (Meyer v. Ewald, 224 NW2d 419, Wis, 1974). A common practice is where the present defendant used the prosecution as a means of collecting a debt (Kitchens v. Barlow, 164 So2d 745, Miss, 1964) or of compelling performance of a contract (Whiteford v. Henthorn, 37 NE 419, Ind, 1893).

''Malice'' is generally a question of fact for the jury, unlike ''probable cause,'' which may be reserved for the court (Giant of Virginia, Inc. v. Pigg, 152 SE2d 271, Va, 1967). ''Malice,'' or improper purpose, may be proved by circumstantial evidence; a serious abuse of authority may per se infer ''malice,'' as in Martin v. City of Albany (396 NYS2d 612, 1977). But a jury is not required to draw the inference that the present defendant was guilty of ''malice'' merely because "probable cause" was lacking. (Cf. Quinlan v. Breslin, 200 A 989, RI, 1938, where "malice" was inferred from lack of probable cause.)

In DeDaviess v. U-Haul Inc. (267 SE2d 633, Ga, 1980) the Georgia Court of Appeals held an attorney liable for malicious prosecution upon finding of "malice" in his pursuit of a criminal course of action to collect a debt in violation of a canon of the Georgia code of ethics. But generally such efforts to predicate liability upon violations of the American Bar Association (ABA) Code of Professional Responsibility, for example, have been unsuccessful (Martin v. Trevino, 578 SW2d 763, Tex, 1978).

Indeed, it has been suggested that the standard of "malice" varies with the jurisdiction and the jurisdiction's predilection for or against the action for malicious prosecution. In Spencer v. Burglass (337 So2d 596, La, 1976) the Louisiana appellate court held that the allegations that the attorney "frivolously filed suit" without any medical evidence of malpractice and without interviewing witnesses or obtaining medical advice did not amount to "malice." The court recounted public policy that demands that citizens be able to seek redress in the courts, but that countersuits and actions for malicious prosecution should be discouraged. The court opined: "At worst, the allegation is that defendant [attorney] went to trial with a poor case and got his just desserts [*sic*], to wit, he lost. If that constitutes malice, the courtrooms are full of malicious attorneys."

4.6 DAMAGES RESULTING FROM PROCEEDING

The fifth element in the cause of action for malicious prosecution (i.e., institution or continuance of prior proceeding, termination of prior proceeding in favor of present plaintiff, absence of probable cause, and malice in instituting or continuing proceeding) is damages resulting from proceeding. No damages are presumed, and the present plaintiff must give proof of any material damage, although in a minority of jurisdictions the English rule as to proof of "special damages" is required. (See the Oregon decision of O'Toole v. Franklin, supra, which identified as of 1977 the following states as following the English rule: District of Columbia, Georgia, Illinois, Iowa, Kentucky, Maryland, New Jersey, New Mexico, New York, North Carolina, Ohio, Oregon, Pennsylvania, Rhode Island, Texas, Washington, and Wisconsin.) Material damages may include increased malpractice insurance premiums, impairment of professional reputation, loss of income due to absence from professional practice occasioned by the lawsuit, mental distress, as well as actual out-of-pocket expenses such as attorney's fees and court costs incurred in defending the groundless, frivolous action.

Since the action for malicious prosecution delineates injury to reputation, damages have generally been permitted in substantial sums of money on the theory that there is also a serious harm in the violation of the present plaintiff's right to freedom from unjustifiable prosecution (Young v. Jack Boring's Inc., 540 SW2d 887, Mo, 1976). Damages have been awarded for myriad reasons, to wit: harm resulting from the impact upon reputation (Sampson v. Hunt, 665 P2d 743, Kan, 1983); harm caused by dispossession or interference with advantageous use of land, including loss of employment (Ex Parte Kimberly-Clark Corp., 449 So2d 794, Ala, 1983); mental suffering or humiliation (Haswell v. Liberty Mutual Insurance Co., 557 SW2d 628, Mo, 1977); and punitive damages (Akin v. Dahl, 661 SW2d 917, Tex, 1983). (Punitive or exemplary damages are permitted under Sections 674 and 677 of Restatement (Second) of Torts.) In California in Babb v. Superior Court (479 P2d 379, 1971), damages included out-of-pocket expenses such as attorneys' and other fees, business losses, general harm to reputation, to social standing, and to credit, as well as mental and bodily harm.

"Special injury" or "special damages" are frequently invoked where the court seeks to curb the action for malicious prosecution, as indicated in the New Jersey decision of Ackerman v. Lagano (412 A2d 1054, 1979), where the court ruled that the physician who brought the action for malicious prosecution had not proven any "special grievance" such as interference with his personal liberty or freedom or that he had sustained damages different from and in addition to ordinary litigation expenses. Without such proof the physician's claim failed, for claimed damages to his professional reputation did not per se qualify as "special injury." The New Jersey court explained that the overriding public policy of free and unfettered access to the courts justified the strict requirement of proof of "special damage" in malicious prosecution actions in New Jersey. A similar view was held by the Kansas Supreme Court in Nelson v. Miller (607 P2d 438, 1980), where the plaintiff physician was sued for medical malpractice by his patient, who was represented by the defendant attorney herein; after the malpractice suit was dismissed without prejudice, plaintiff sued the attorney for malicious prosecution on the ground that the prior malpractice suit was instituted without "probable cause." But the trial court favored the defendant attorney, in that plaintiff had failed to allege "special damages" from the prior malpractice action, and furthermore there was no privity between the plaintiff and the defendant.

4.7 DEFENSES TO MALICIOUS PROSECUTION

Probably the most popular defense to the action of malicious prosecution is proof that the present plaintiff was in fact guilty of the very same offense with which he was first charged (Clary v. Hale, 175 Cal App2d 880, 1959). In other words, the prior legal proceeding is retried or re-evaluated by the instant court. The defensive burden of proof is upon the present defendant that the present plaintiff is at least guilty of a substantially equivalent tort or crime. (See Patterson v. Brogan, 198 SE2d 586, SC, 1973.)

In Bain v. Phillips (228 SE2d 576, Va, 1976) the present plaintiff filed a mechanic's lien against the present defendant for conduct arising out of a business transaction. Subsequently, the present defendant, allegedly upon advice of counsel, instituted a prosecution against the present plaintiff for violation of a "fictitious name statute." Counsel for the present plaintiff informed the present defendant that continued prosecution of the statutory violation would be frivolous since the present plaintiff was clearly not covered by the statute. But the present defendant continued to press charges, and after charges of violation of statute were dropped, suit for malicious prosecution was commenced. The trial court ruled that the present defendant lacked "probable cause" as a matter of law, despite the defense argument of a mistake of law and of fact. The Virginia Supreme Court agreed with the trial court, pointing out that the present defendant could not, as a matter of law, have harbored under a reasonable mistake of law or of fact his decision to prosecute, acting as he did upon skimpy facts and mere assertions of law from persons other than attorneys.

It should be noted that an action for malicious prosecution is generally restricted to a short statute of limitations, as illustrated by Section 215 (3) of the New York Civil Practice Law and Rules (CPLR), which requires the New York action to be commenced within one year. But the claim does not accrue until judgment is entered in the prior legal proceeding. (Interestingly, in New York, abuse of process has a three-year statute of limitations under Section 214 of CPLR.)

In Jackson v. Jackson (201 SE2d 722, NC, 1974) plaintiff sued his wife, from whom he was separated, and allegedly one of the partners of the law firm representing the wife "conspired" with her to institute criminal proceedings against the husband, charging him with attempting to burn a dwelling house and two automobiles. The plaintiff-husband was arrested but never tried, and the charges were "nolle prossed." The North Carolina Court of Appeals answered the single question "whether all partners in the law firm are liable for a malicious prosecution instituted upon the advice of one partner but without the participation, authorization, knowledge, or approval of other partners." The court affirmed the ruling of the trial court that vicarious liability was not applicable because malicious prosecution was not "within the ordinary course of business of a law partnership."

According to the Illinois Supreme Court in Stopka v. Lesser (402 NE2d 781, 1980), there were between 1948 and 1980 a total of 191 cases of malicious prosecution tried in Illinois, and only 8 cases were successful.

4.8 PRIVILEGED COMPLAINTS TO BAR ASSOCIATION

Traditionally, as exemplified by the New Jersey case of Toft v. Ketchum (113 A2d 671, 1955), there was absolute immunity to complainants to state bar associations from malicious prosecution actions. Here an attorney sued the complainant for maliciously filing a false complaint about the attorney with the local ethics and grievance committee; the complaint accused the plaintiff attorney of unethical conduct in certain real estate transactions wherein the attorney acted as a real estate broker. The bar association committee dismissed the petition on the ground that the complaint should have been directed to the real estate commission and not to the bar association. The New Jersey Court of Appeals decided that the public interest outweighed the attorney's need for protection against malicious complaints and upheld the lower court's judgment of dismissal of the malicious prosecution action. The court opined that public policy required that the filing of such complaints before bar associations should be absolutely privileged: "[It] is only through the cooperation of those with knowledge of unethical conduct of an attorney that the Court is made aware of such conduct as requires action on its part. It is in the public interest to encourage those with information to come forward, free from the threat of malicious prosecution." The dissenting opinion argued against absolute immunity which can only "serve to encourage the use of disciplinary proceedings as privileged sanctuaries to carry out personal vendettas." The next year the New Jersey legislature (NJ Stat Ann, Section 2A:47A-1) mandated the end of the absolute privilege. In the 1980 decision of Friedland v. Podhoretz (415 A2d 381) the New Jersey Superior Court upheld the constitutionality of the statute authorizing an attorney's malicious prosecution action against the complainant to a bar association.

In the state of New York it would appear that the complainant to the local bar association is entitled to the defense of absolute privilege, as illustrated by Sullivan v. Crisona (283 NYS2d 62, 1967). The second cause of action in this libel action was for malicious prosecution arising out of charges brought against an attorney before a local grievance committee. In Florida a client filed a letter with the state bar association claiming that his attorney improperly commingled his personal funds with those of his law firm's clients. The bar association found no probable cause, and the attorney thereupon instituted a malicious prosecution action against the client. The Florida Court of Appeals in Stone v. Rosen (348 So2d 387, 1977) affirmed summary judgment in favor of the client on the ground that complaints to bar associations are absolutely privileged. In California in Stanwyck v. Horne (146 Cal App3d 450, 1983) the appellate court opined that, as a matter of public policy, complainants to bar associations should not be subject to actions for malicious prosecution, and that such immunity (or privilege) promotes public confidence in the law profession by permitting public access with impunity to the clients of lawyers who initiate the policing of lawyers. The court pointed out that the attorney is afforded ample protection by bar association procedures to see that the attorney is not exposed to unwarranted publicity where groundless charges are made:

> The procedure . . . is well adapted to provide reasonable protection for both the public and members of the bar. The State Bar will accept a complaint from any member of the public who feels, whether rightly or wrongly, that he has been aggrieved by the action of an attorney. . . . These complaints are confidential unless they result in disciplinary

> action taken against the attorney. . . . This procedure acts as a safety valve for the public. It thereby is made to feel that the law profession is not a closed body which protects its members no matter how unfaithful to their trusts any might be, and which would punish a member of the public who makes an unfounded charge by disclosure of his name and his charge. . . . The procedure and its confidential character is a great protection to the lawyer. He is not exposed to publicity where groundless charges are made. In some of the cases, the charges are so meritless that the attorney is not contacted for his explanation. The fact that a charge has been made against an attorney no matter how guiltless the attorney may be, if generally known, would do irreparable harm even though he be cleared by the State Bar.

The privilege (or absolute immunity) afforded complainants to bar associations is somewhat matched by the principle of the application to other private complainants before any administrative tribunal, to wit: a cause of action for malicious prosecution of an administrative proceeding will not lie in the absence of the complainant's flagrant and egregious abuse of the administrative procedure which results in substantial harm to the prosecuted attorney. (See generally 12 *San Fernando Valley Law Review* 77, 1984). In White v. Towers (235 P2d 209, Cal, 1951) the California Supreme Court had made it clear that the law does not favor actions for malicious prosecution; here the defendant investigator for the California State Fish and Game Commission had allegedly instituted maliciously criminal proceedings against the plaintiff by the commission. The court in affirming a lower court judgment sustained a demurrer without leave to amend.

In 1982 the California Supreme Court in In Re Marriage of Flaherty (646 P2d 179) undertook to define "frivolous" for the purpose of determining whether sanctions should be imposed upon an attorney for an unsuccessful appeal. The standard was not whether the attorney's arguments on appeal were unsuccessful but whether any reasonable attorney would agree that to assert that position on appeal was totally and completely without merit. In Pennsylvania attorneys must adhere to a standard of liability as set forth in a statute for an attorney who acts in a "grossly negligent manner" (42 Pa Cons Stat Ann, Section 8351); the successful plaintiff could be the client's adversary!

5

Wrongful Civil Proceedings

The action for malicious prosecution, as delineated herein in Chapter 4, began as a remedy for unjustifiable *criminal* proceedings, but the action has undergone a process of extension into *civil* proceedings as well. To encompass the multitudes of civil proceedings such as quasi-criminal proceedings which involve interference with the person as in the case of proceedings in lunacy, bastardy, or juvenile delinquency, inter alia (Alexander v. Alexander, 229 F2d 111, 4th Cir, 1956; Coffey v. Myers, 84 Id 105, 1882; and see generally 22 *Minnesota Law Review* 1060, 1938), the tort of wrongful civil proceedings, or wrongful use of civil proceedings, has been utilized. But the action for wrongful civil proceedings differs in some respects from the action for malicious prosecution in the following particulars: (1) there need not be a favorable termination of prior legal proceedings (as delineated herein at §4.3), as illustrated in Blankenship v. Staton (348 SW2d 925, Ky, 1961), where an attachment ancillary to the civil suit was wrongful, or as illustrated by Rossiter v. Minnesota B-S Paper Co. (33 NW 855, Minn, 1887) where a bond was filed for the release of attached property; (2) "probable cause" standard (described at §4.4 herein) is more readily upheld so that the present defendant's past conduct in initiating or continuing the prior civil proceeding can be based on significantly less certain knowledge or information, as shown in Hoffman v. Kimmel (20 P2d 393, Ore, 1933); in Standley v. Western Auto Supply Co. (319 SW2d 924, Mo, 1959) the court found "probable cause" even though the suit was brought on a claim discharged in bankruptcy, because it was always possible that the defense of bankruptcy might be waived; (3) "malice" or improper purpose requisite (described at §4.5 herein) is relaxed in favor of simple ill-will or simply lack of belief in any possible success of the action, as shown in

Robinson v. Godchaux's (307 So2d 287, La, 1975), where the plaintiff customer sued the department store for sending out a bill after the bill had been paid, and where no proof of spite was found, yet "malice" was held to exist; (4) the instigator or person who continues the prior legal proceeding is less harshly penalized for a mistake of law, as demonstrated in Comment e of Section 675 of Restatement (Second) of Torts; and (5) damages for reputation (delineated at §4.6 herein) are not readily awarded, unless in the wrongful lunacy or bankruptcy proceeding reputation is seriously put into issue, according to Comment c of Section 681 of Restatement (Second) of Torts. Section 681 sets forth the cause of action for wrongful civil proceedings by providing that plaintiff is entitled to recover for

> (a) the harm normally resulting from any arrest or imprisonment, or any dispossession or interference with the advantageous use of his land, chattels, or other things suffered by him during the course of the proceedings, and (b) the harm to his reputation by any defamatory matter alleged as the basis of the proceedings, and (c) the expense that he has reasonably incurred in defending himself against the proceedings, and (d) any emotional distress that is caused by the proceedings. . . .

In Landmark Holding Corp. v. Bermant (664 F2d 891, 2nd Cir, 1981) plaintiff partners in real estate brought an antitrust suit, alleging that defendants, owners of two existing shopping centers, as well as others, had "conspired" to prevent plaintiffs from opening a competing shopping center by organizing protracted opposition before Connecticut administrative agencies, by litigating in bad faith in Connecticut courts, and by soliciting and subsidizing others to bring baseless litigation in Connecticut courts. The federal district court dismissed the complaint, but the Second U.S. Court of Appeals reversed and remanded upon the ground that the First Amendment's free speech did not "shield" the activities of the defendants since the conduct of the defendants fell within the "sham exception," as described in Eastern Railroads Presidents Conference v. Noerr Motor Freight, Inc. (365 US 127, 1961), wherein the U.S. Supreme Court held that such attempts might be actionable under the antitrust laws where they are a "mere sham to cover what is actually nothing more than an attempt to interfere directly with the business relations of a competitor." The wrongful civil proceedings were here highlighted by the "unethical conduct in the setting of the adjudicatory process," by the pursuit of "a pattern of baseless, repetitive claims," and by the abuse of process "effectively barring . . . access to the agencies and courts." According to the court,

> the activities alleged, if credited, show that the Plaza defendants conspired to prevent the plaintiffs from erecting a competing shopping center. In furtherance of this conspiracy, the Plaza defendants appealed to the Court of Common Pleas and Connecticut Supreme Court from each decision of the HPZC (Hamden Planning and Zoning Commission), knowing that they lacked standing to do so. These defendants had no reasonable hopes of winning these appeals, only of securing delay. Each such appeal was

dismissed, as were most of the landowner appeals solicited and financed by the Plaza defendants. Furthermore, the Plaza defendants deliberately protracted the proceedings by misrepresenting to the Chief Justice of the Connecticut Supreme Court that they needed extra time to have the record printed; among themselves, they acknowledged this request to be "purely bull." Finally, an attorney representing both the Plaza defendants and the Neals failed to communicate a settlement offer from the plaintiffs to the Neals. Acceptance of this offer by the Neals would have removed a major obstacle to the rapid resolution of the remaining appeals before the Connecticut Supreme Court. In sum, by the bringing of numerous meritless appeals, by deliberate delay in the prosecution of those appeals, by the solicitation and subsidization of meritless litigation by the landowners, and by their attorney's failure to convey a settlement offer to the Neals, the Plaza defendants successfully stalled plaintiff's applications for zoning changes on the Evergreen Avenue property for five years. This delay ultimately forced the plaintiffs to abandon their venture. We hold that these allegations state a cause of action under the antitrust laws. The right to petition the courts for the redress of grievances does not protect abuse of the judicial process through the institution and subsidization of baseless litigation and delay. . . .

The lone dissent pointed out that

[t]he First Amendment guarantees access to our nation's courts regardless of the plaintiff's anti-competitive motivation. Unless the plaintiff's conduct corrupts the judicial processes, California Motor Transport Co. v. Trucking Unlimited, 404 U.S. 508, 513, 92 S. Ct. 609, 613, 30 L. Ed.2d 642, (1972), or deprives a competitor of meaningful access to adjudicatory tribunals, id. at 512, 92 S Ct. at 612, he is not in violation of the Sherman Act. Wilmorite, Inc. v. Eagan Real Estate, Inc., supra, 454 F. Supp. at 1131. Sham litigation may perhaps corrupt the judicial process. However, a case in which the Connecticut Supreme Court has seen fit to grant certification can hardly be described as "sham." See State v. Cullum, 149 Conn. 728, 176 A.2d 587, (1961); Conn. Practice Book §761C. This would surely seem to be true where, as in the instant case, a twelve page opinion, Schwartz v. Town of Hamden, 168 Conn. 8, 357 A.2d 488 1975, and a seven page opinion, Schwartz v. Town of Hamden, 168 Conn. 20, 357 A.2d 496, 1975, follow the granting of review.

I do not believe that the alleged improper conduct of defendants' attorneys rose, or perhaps "fell" is a better word, to the level of such "illegal and reprehensible" practices as perjury, fraud, and bribery, so as to corrupt and make illegal the entire judicial process in which defendants were engaged. . . .

. . . So far as appears, the administrative and judicial proceedings in Connecticut were fairly conducted. Plaintiffs had their day in court and prevailed. Plaintiffs' real complaint, one that is voiced all too often today, is that they had too many days in court. Relief from inordinate delay should have been sought in the Connecticut tribunals to which plaintiffs had ready access. While their plight merits sympathy, it does not merit invocation of the Sherman Act.

6

False Arrest or False Imprisonment

6.1 FALSE ARREST AS A TORT

The tort of false arrest arises out of an unlawful detention by police over a person or persons resulting in a restraint of his or their liberty. False arrest is technically distinguished from false imprisonment, but a private person can also falsely arrest another person without making an official arrest. False arrest may exist entirely apart from the tort of false imprisonment or from any purported process of law enforcement (Bender v. City of Seattle, 664 P2d 492, Wash, 1983). False arrest is generally committed only by one who has legal authority to arrest, or who pretends to have legal authority to arrest (Children v. Burton, 331 NW2d 673, Iowa, 1983). A person legally arrested may be falsely imprisoned if there is an unreasonable delay in taking him before a magistrate or court, or if he is detained when he has a right to be released. See generally 43 *Connecticut Bar Journal* 598 (1969).

The basic elements of the tort of false arrest encompass the detention of the plaintiff and the unlawfulness of such detention; neither malice (Fontenot v. Lavergne, 365 So2d 1168, La, 1978) nor lack of probable cause (Tumbarella v. Kroger Co., 271 NW2d, 284, Mich, 1978) is required. In Davis v. City of Syracuse the New York Court of Appeals on November 14, 1985, analyzed municipal liability for false arrest. Here a complainant filed a police report with the municipality alleging that plaintiff Davis had assaulted him in his apartment. Almost two months later a city judge signed an order for Davis to appear in court two weeks in the future; Davis did not make the court appearance, so a bench warrant for his arrest was issued. About six months later plaintiff Davis was arrested. He protested his innocence, denied that he had assaulted the complainant, and asserted that he was forty years of age, not thirty-one, as stated on the warrant. Nevertheless, Davis spent the night in a police cell and was released eighteen hours later pending trial. One month later, after complainant confirmed that Davis was not the assaulter, the court granted the prosecutor's motion to dismiss the indictment. Davis then filed notice of claim against the municipality and commenced the action for false arrest and false imprisonment. A jury awarded Davis $10,000 in damages, but the highest New York court reversed and opined:

A detention, otherwise unlawful, is privileged where the confinement was by arrest under a valid process issued by a court having jurisdiction (Restatement, 2nd Torts §35, comment a; Prosser, Torts (4th ed), §11) (Broughton v. State of NY, 37 NY2d 451; Boose v. City of Rochester, 71 AD2d 59, 66 (Simons, J.)). A qualification to this rule has been applied in the so-called "misnomer cases," where warrants could have been applied with complete accuracy to two or more persons (Williams v. City of Buffalo, 72 AD2d 952; Craner v. Corbett, 27 AD2d 796; Maracle v. State of NY, 50 Misc., 2d, 348). In such cases, the officer has been required to exercise reasonable care in assuring that he has arrested the person intended to be apprehended under the warrant. To be contrasted is the situation, presented here, where the plaintiff is the person intended to be arrested and the only person to whom the warrant could validly be applied (see Boose v. City of Rochester, 71 AD2d 59, 67, supra). The warrant in this case could validly support the arrest of one person alone—the plaintiff, David Davis residing at 135 Randall Avenue. Unlike the misnomer cases where error is committed by the police in failing properly to execute a warrant, the error here was in the issuance of a warrant that, based on information supplied by the District Attorney, named a person other than the person who was in fact accused of the crime (see Boose v. City of Rochester, supra [negligent police investigation prior to issuance of warrant resulted in the naming in the warrant of a person other than the actual suspect]). In executing this warrant, Officer Pendergast was obliged only to assure himself that he was arresting the person described therein, and that the description bore a reasonable resemblance to the arrestee.

A contrary view by the New York Court of Appeals in 1974 was Smith v. County of Nassau (311 NE2d 489), where Judge Rabin opined:

It is clear that plaintiff made out a prima facie case for false arrest and false imprisonment by showing that defendant's police officer intentionally arrested and confined him against his consent, and without lawful privilege of a warrant (see, e. g., 1 Harper and James, Law of Torts §§3.6-3.7, pp. 224-226; 1 Cooley, Torts (rth ed.), §109; Prosser, Torts (3rd ed.), §12; Restatement, 2nd Torts, §35). Because the arrest and imprisonment were effected without a warrant, a presumption arises that both are unlawful, and the burden of proving justification, including "reasonable cause," is cast upon the defendant (Woodson v. New York City Housing Auth., 10 N.Y.2d 30, 33, 217 N.Y.S.2d 31, 32, 176 N.E.2d 57, 58 . . .).

The requirement that an officer have reasonable cause for a warrantless arrest represents a compromise, with its roots deep in the common law, between the individual's interest in personal liberty and society's competing interest in its own protection through the apprehension of criminals. . . . Where such cause exists, and a felony has been committed, a police officer is justified in arresting without a warrant, irrespective of the innocence of the person arrested. While this compromise may occasionally subject law-abiding persons to inconvenience or hardship, "any more lax rules would be greatly dangerous to the peace of the community and make the escape of criminals frequent and easy." (Burns v. Erben 40 N.Y. 463, 470).

Reasonable cause will, of course, vary according to the circumstances and exigencies of each particular case and as a consequence a "tight, inclusive definition is neither necessary nor desirable." (People v. Coffey, 12 N.Y.2d 443, 451, 240 N.Y.S.2d 721, 725, 191 N.E.2d 263, 266). Good faith alone is not enough. . . . In addition to good faith, there must be reasonable ground for the officer's belief that the person to be arrested committed the felony. In Coffey Chief Judge Desmond approved the following formulation for reasonable cause (6 C.J.S., Arrest, §6, p. 596) which we reaffirm: "Where an officer, in good faith, believes that a person is guilty of a felony, and his belief rests on such grounds as would induce an ordinarily prudent and cautious man, under the circumstances, to believe likewise, he has such probable cause for his belief as would justify him in arresting without a warrant." . . .

Applying this test to the facts before us: would an ordinarily prudent and cautious person, under the circumstances known to the officer, have made the arrest upon Pugh's identification, without delaying to procure a warrant?

There was no indication whatever that plaintiff was fleeing or would attempt to flee during the time it would have taken to obtain a warrant. Nor was there any other exigency which might have advised the officer against taking the time to seek out a Magistrate to issue a warrant.

We conclude that these are facts from which reasonable men might draw different inferences, particularly on the crucial issue of the reasonableness of the officer's complete reliance upon the identification to support his belief that plaintiff had committed the felony. Taking into account the circumstances known to the officer at the time of the arrest, we cannot say that as a matter of law the officer's reliance upon Pugh's identification was reasonable; or, stated differently, that Pugh's identification constituted, as a matter of law, such grounds as would induce an ordinarily prudent and cautious person, under the circumstances, to believe that plaintiff had committed the felony.

According to the *New York Times* (January 19, 1986, at p. 16) a Boston graduate student was arrested at gunpoint while getting out of an automobile that he was driving; the police had reason to believe that the car plaintiff was driving was a stolen car. Plaintiff was held in jail overnight, and a week later he was found not guilty and furthermore that no crime had been committed, for the car was not stolen. Subsequently, Suke Omere Emma filed suit in the federal district court charging the Boston police with violating his civil rights against false arrest and false imprisonment. The defense admitted faulty computer data and a failure to correct the misinformation about the automobile which plaintiff's cousin and roommate owned and which automobile plaintiff had been driving with his cousin's permission.

The defense of privilege to false arrest is illustrated by the right of a business or merchant to detain or restrain a person for reasonable investigation where the defendant reasonably suspects the person has committed a tort or crime. In Bonkowski v. Arlan's Department Store (162 NW2d 347, Mich, 1968) plaintiff, suspected of shoplifting, was detained by defendant merchant's detective outside the store until she revealed the contents of her purse. When plaintiff produced sales slips for the items, the detective let her go. The Michigan Court of Appeals sanctioned the merchant's privilege to detain or restrain as a defense to the action for false arrest, even where the suspect has left the premises of the store.

Where a person goes voluntarily with a police officer to the police station to clear up a matter, there is no arrest which can form the basis for an action for false arrest (Pollack v. City of Newark, 147 F Supp 35, NJ, 1956, aff 248 F2d 543, 3rd Cir, 1957; cert den 355 US 964, 1959; reh den 362 US 907, 1960). The presence of a policeman who questions the plaintiff without the policeman purporting to exercise the authority to arrest by taking the plaintiff into custody is not a false arrest (Hill v. Taylor, 15 NW 899, Mich, 1883).

Generally the statute of limitations for an action for false arrest is short, like the one-year New York statute in Section 215 (3) of the Civil Practice Law and Rules. In Caminito v. City of New York (45 Misc2d 241, 1971) the court excused the plaintiff because noncompliance with the statute of limitations was caused by the defendant's conduct in unlawfully placing plaintiff under arrest!

6.2 FALSE IMPRISONMENT HISTORICALLY

The old action of trespass is said to have sired the actions of false arrest and false imprisonment, for both actions protect the personal interests in freedom from restraint of movement and from detention. According to Blackstone, "every confinement of a person is an imprisonment whether it be in a common prison, or in a private house, or in the stocks, or even forcibly detaining one in the public street" (3 *Blackstone Commentaries* 127, 1790). The confinement or detention must be total, as illustrated by a 1945 English case, Bird v. Jones (115 E.R. 668 Q.B.). Here defendant had blocked off part of a public road and used it to seat spectators at a boat race; plaintiff wanted to walk through this side of the road and was stopped by the defendant, but plaintiff succeeded in climbing over the enclosed area until he was halted by two policemen who told him to turn around and go back so as to avoid the entire area. Plaintiff sued defendant for false imprisonment, but the English court ruled that there can be no false imprisonment when plaintiff's movement was restrained in only one direction:

> [C]ompelling a man to go in a given direction against his will may amount to imprisonment. But I cannot bring my mind to the conclusion that, if one man merely obstructs

the passage of another in a particular direction, whether by threat of personal violence or otherwise, leaving him at liberty to stay where he is or to go in any other direction if he pleases, he can be said thereby to imprison him. He does him wrong, undoubtedly, if there was a right to pass in that direction, and would be liable to an action on the case for obstructing the passage, or of assault, if, on the party persisting in going in that direction, he touched his person, or so threatened him as to amount to an assault. But imprisonment is, as I apprehend, a total restraint of the liberty of the person, for however short a time, and not a partial obstruction of his will, whatever inconvenience it may bring on him. The quality of the act cannot, however, depend on the right of the opposite party. If it be an imprisonment to prevent a man passing along the public highway, it must be equally so to prevent him passing further along a field into which he has broken by a clear act of trespass. . . .

The action for false imprisonment, derived from the action of trespass, may be maintained without proof of actual damages, but the successful plaintiff must be aware of the confinement, for it is the restraint or detention that constitutes the tort, as illustrated by the 1834 English case of Herring v. Boyle (149 Eng Rep 1126). Section 42 of the Restatement (Second) of Torts supports that view, but it would appear that the requisite of awareness of confinement does not explain why a baby, lunatic, or incompetent should be denied protection from false imprisonment simply because of lack of awareness of confinement (55 *Columbia Law Review* 847, 1955).

6.3 CHARACTER OF THE CONFINEMENT OR DETENTION

Section 35 of Restatement (Second) of Torts delineates false imprisonment in terms of the character of the actor and of the act itself:

§35. False Imprisonment

(1) An actor is subject to liability to another for false imprisonment if
 (a) he acts intending to confine the other or a third person within boundaries fixed by the actor, and
 (b) his act directly or indirectly results in such confinement of the other, and
 (c) the other is conscious of the confinement or is harmed by it.

(2) An act which is not done with the intention stated in Subsection (1,a) does not make the actor liable to the other for a merely transitory or otherwise harmless confinement, although the act involves an unreasonable risk of imposing it and therefore, would be negligent or reckless if the risk threatened bodily harm.

The intentional nature of the tort is illustrated by Whittaker v. Sanford (85 A 399, Me, 1912), where the female plaintiff agreed to travel on defendant's yacht across the Atlantic Ocean on condition that the male defendant would not attempt to detain her on board for any purpose, particularly not try to re-convert her to the religious movement with which defendant was affiliated. Upon arrival in port in the state of Maine, defendant refused to furnish a boat so that she was detained on his yacht for over a month. The Maine Supreme Judicial Court supported her claim of false imprisonment, even though defendant exerted no physical force on her but intentionally obstructed her from leaving the confined area. The court also predicated false imprisonment upon defendant's breach of duty to take active measures to release plaintiff. Clearly the male defendant intended to and did confine the female plaintiff with more than "moral pressure." False imprisonment exists where one's freedom of motion is surrendered because of force directed at the person or his property (Griffin v. Clark, 42 P2d 297, Ida, 1935).

The requisite that the detainee be "conscious of the confinement" under Section 35 (c) of Restatement (Second) of Torts was examined in Parvi v. City of Kingston (362 NE2d 960, NY, 1977). Here the plaintiff was found by police in an intoxicated condition. He told the defendant police that he had nowhere to go; and so rather than place him under arrest, the police drove him out of the city to an abandoned golf course to "sleep it off." Later plaintiff sued the police for false imprisonment, contending that he was confined against his will, although he could not recall whether he was conscious of being confined at the time he was taken out of town. After the trial court dismissed his complaint, the New York Court of Appeals ruled that it was not necessary to show plaintiff's present recollection of previous consciousness of confinement in order to make out a prima facie case of false imprisonment. The court opined that he would not be entitled to recover if he had not been aware of confinement at the time it occurred; the fact that alcohol or the injuries that he sustained precluded his recollection is immaterial if indeed he was conscious of the confinement at the time of the confinement. The fact that he was responsive to the police order, had conversation with the police in the police car, and that he actually on his own requested to be let off at the golf course, attested to his consciousness at the time of confinement. The dissenting opinion of Chief Judge Charles Breitel was based on evidence that plaintiff had no memory of the entire incident and admitted that his only knowledge of the incident followed subsequent conversations with the police.

Fear accompanied by threats of harm to person or property may or may not give rise to false imprisonment. In Rougeau v. Firestone Tire & Rubber Co. (274 So2d 454, La, 1973) plaintiff employee was suspected of stealing two lawnmowers belonging to his employer; three corporate employees and the plaintiff went to plaintiff's house to search for the missing property; but plaintiff, upon the advice of his attorney, refused to allow the search. At the plant plaintiff was asked by defendants to wait in the guardhouse with two guards. Thirty minutes later when plaintiff became ill, he voluntarily left the confines of the corporate guardhouse. The Louisiana appellate court found no false imprisonment for "at no time was he totally restrained. . . . Additionally, plaintiff never revealed to anyone that he did not want to stay in the guardhouse, thus showing his implied consent to stay." In Faniel v. Chesapeake and Potomac Telephone Co. (404 A2d 147, DC, 1979) plaintiff employee was questioned by security officers of the defendant employer regarding the existence of an illegal telephone in her home. The questioning occurred in the corporate conference room during regular working hours and in the presence of her supervisor. After plaintiff admitted to possession of the illegal phone, the security officers informed her that they were taking her to her home to recover the missing property, and plaintiff did not appear to object. The trial court nevertheless accepted a jury verdict in favor of the plaintiff; the appellate court in the District of Columbia reversed, holding that there was no evidence that plaintiff had yielded to threats, express or implied, or to physical force; mere questioning while at work did not constitute a detention, nor did the detour in the automobile while on the way to plaintiff's home to pick up the illegal telephone. In point of fact, plaintiff failed to negate her prior consent to the entire incident; the fear of losing her job, while a strong incentive, did not render her behavior involuntary for the purposes of false imprisonment. Comment c of Section 36 of Restatement (Second) of Torts should be noted: "If the actor by force or threats of force, or by exerting legal authority, compels another to accompany him from place to place, he has as effectively confined the other as though he had locked him in a room."

Escaping from confinement can sometimes involve personal injuries, as illustrated in Sindle v. New York City Transit Authority (307 NE2d 245, NYS, 1973). Here a fourteen-year-old boy was injured when he fell under the wheels of defendant's bus as he attempted to climb out of the bus after the bus driver had locked the doors to prevent all the suspected vandals from escaping. The bus was on its way to the police station. The trial court denied defendant the opportunity to amend its answer to the complaint of false imprisonment by pleading the defense of justification. The New York Court of Appeals opined that "it was an abuse of discretion for the trial court to deny the motion to amend and to exclude the evidence of justification. It was the defendant's burden to prove justification—a defense that a plaintiff in an action for false imprisonment should be prepared to meet. . . . " The court then outlined "some of the considerations relevant to the issue of justification":

> [G]enerally, restraint or detention, reasonable under the circumstances and in time and manner, imposed for the purpose of preventing another from inflicting personal injuries or interfering with or damaging real or personal property in one's lawful possession or custody is not unlawful. . . . Also, a parent, guardian or teacher entrusted with the care or supervision of a child may use physical force reasonably necessary to maintain discipline or promote the welfare of the child. . . . Similarly, a school bus driver, entrusted with the care of his student-passengers and the custody of public property, has the duty to take reasonable measures for the safety and protection of both—the passengers and the property. In this regard, the reasonableness of his actions—as bearing on the defense of justification—is to be determined from a consideration of all the circumstances. At a minimum, this would seem to import, a consideration of the need to protect the persons and property in his charge, the duty to aid the investigation and

apprehension of those inflicting damage, the manner and place of the occurrence, and the feasibility and practicality of other alternative courses of action.

Furthermore, the court ruled that a person who is allegedly falsely imprisoned is not relieved of the duty of reasonable care for his own safety in extricating himself from the unlawful detention.

6.4 ELEMENTS OF INTENT AND MOTIVE

Since false imprisonment is an intentional tort, the intent and motive of the defendant are of prime importance. The defendant must know or realize that, due to his action or inaction, confinement of the plaintiff must result. In Roberts v. Hecht Co. (280 F Supp 639, Md, 1968) the federal district court in Maryland scrutinized the conduct of the defendant department store in its efforts to curb shoplifting, noting in particular Section 120A of Restatement (Second) of Torts, which provides:

> Temporary Detention for Investigation
>
> One who reasonably believes that another has tortiously taken a chattel upon his premises, or has failed to make due cash payment for a chattel purchased or services rendered there, is privileged, without arresting the other, to detain him on the premises for the time necessary for a reasonable investigation of the facts.

The court then commented:

> What constitutes "justification" for the temporary detention of a suspected shoplifter under the Maryland law as it now stands is not clear. Probable cause is ordinarily an important element of such justification. . . . Where the probable cause is strong enough, it may be equivalent to justification, as where the merchant or his duly authorized employee sees the suspect take a garment off a rack and put it in her bag. In the instant case the detectives did not see plaintiff take the pants off a rack or off a table, and did not see any tags on the pants while plaintiff was in the fitting room. Nevertheless, plaintiff's actions in the sportswear department and in the fitting room, particularly putting the pants in a paper bag, justified suspicion on the part of the detectives.
>
> The Court finds and concludes that there was probable cause for detaining plaintiff on the premises for the time necessary to make a reasonable investigation of the facts, as the term "probable cause" is used in the Maryland cases. The Court finds and concludes that there was no justification for such detention, as the term "justification" is used in the Maryland cases. Under the present Maryland law, the probable cause may be considered only in mitigation of damages. No malice has been shown.

The opposite view was taken by a federal district court in Florida in Meadows v. F. W. Woolworth Co. (254 F Supp 907, 1966) under the Florida shoplifting statute (Fla Stats Section 811.022(1)), which provided that a "merchant's employee who has probable cause for believing that goods . . . have been unlawfully taken by a person and that he can recover them by taking the person into custody, may, for the purpose of attempting to effect such recovery, take the person into custody, and detain him in a reasonable manner for a reasonable length of time. Such taking into custody . . . shall not render such . . . merchant's employee criminally or civilly liable for . . . false imprisonment.'' Here the defendant store manager had received word from the police that there were ''organized shoplifting activities by teenage girls in the area.'' On the day in question he observed three teenage girls in the vicinity of a counter where two hair pieces were missing; he called to them outside the store, and asked ''if he could look in their purses.'' The three teenagers apparently complied with this request, and after examining two of the three purses he ''discontinued the search.'' The court thereupon concluded:

> Under Florida law the restraint of a person giving rise to false imprisonment can be accomplished by threats as well as force. . . .
>
> All of the testimony here is in accord that there were no threats made nor can the Court find any such inference in any activities at the time and place. Therefore, the restraint element, if here at all, would necessarily reside in a compulsion of a teenage girl by an adult to ''come here.'' . . .
>
> The Court determines that there is no genuine issue as to any material fact here and that the defendant is entitled to judgment as a matter of law, . . . it affirmatively appearing that the manager, Wingate, did indeed have probable cause for momentarily detaining the subject plaintiffs for searching and interrogating in an attempt to recover articles reasonably thought by him to have been unlawfully taken. The momentary detention was certainly reasonable in time and the searching of the pocketbooks was clearly accomplished without any objection on the part of the two girls involved.

It should be observed that shoplifting statutes apply to detentions of suspected shoplifters, not to the arrests of suspected shoplifters, as shown in Cervantez v. J. C. Penney Co. (595 P2d 975, Cal, 1979), where an off-duty ''moonlighting'' police officer was held to the standard of a private person in making the arrest. A train conductor, who detained the plaintiff who had fallen and broke his leg while attempting to leave the train, was guilty of false imprisonment, even though he argued that the law required him to have the injured plaintiff fill out a statement about the accident. The Kansas court in Whitman v. Atchison, T. & S. F. Railroad Co. (116 P 234, 1911) held that the involuntary delay of twenty minutes in getting medical help while plaintiff was in considerable pain constituted the unlawful confinement; the conductor as a private citizen must bear the legal responsibility for his conduct as he intentionally confined the plaintiff.

One aspect of intent and motive to confine is the so-called doctrine of ''transferred intent,'' which predicates liability upon the defendant where another person not intended to be confined by the defendant is actually confined, as where defendant locks the doors of a building in the belief that he is confining A but confines B because A was not in the building. His intent is said to be "transferred" and the defendant is liable for confinement of B. (See Wood v. Cummings, 83 NE 318, Mass, 1908.)

False imprisonment is also actionable where an arrested person is not taken promptly before a court or a magistrate, as illustrated by Nelson v. City of Las Vegas (665 P2d 1141, Nev, 1983).

6.5 DAMAGES

As in the instance of other intentional torts, the tort of false imprisonment may recover nominal damages even if the plaintiff has suffered no actual physical or mental harm (Mason v. Wrightson, 109 A2d 128, Md, 1954). Plaintiff may also recover compensation for loss of time, for mental suffering, humiliation, or similar reputational injuries (Boies v. Raynor, 361 P2d 1, Ariz, 1961). Indeed, all consequential injuries or harms are recoverable including such unusual damages as the theft of plaintiff's automobile while he was being arrested, as in Whitehead v. Stringer (180 P 486, Wash, 1919).

Punitive damages are also available as where the defendant intended the confinement and knew it was unlawful at the time of the confinement, as in Rustici v. Weidemeyer (673 SW2d 762, Mo, 1984).

In Fisher v. State of New York, the New York Court of Claims on January 16, 1986, awarded judgment in the amount of $750,000 to the plaintiff, who served eleven years in prison and fourteen years on parole for a manslaughter conviction until the conviction was overturned for "prosecutorial misconduct." Judge Rossetti examined at length plaintiff's efforts to obtain monetary compensation for the damages he suffered as a result of his erroneous conviction. The plaintiff had obtained in 1984 a special or private legislative act authorizing the Court of Claims to hear claims for unjust conviction and unjust imprisonment. On the following issues the court responded: (1) loss of earnings: "approximately $125,000 in damages"; (2) injuries arising from state malpractice and negligence in prison: "we do not find these typical damages within the purview of the Act"; (3) attorneys' fees: "recovery of legal expenses after indictment requires a finding of malice "which was not shown"; (4) damages for "the indignities and the shame and humiliation and loss of liberty and civil rights and the degradation and loss of reputation and the mental anguish suffered by claimant as a result of and in connection with the erroneous conviction and imprisonment"; and the court replied, "His reputation has suffered much injury by his own hand"; and (5):

> As to psychological damages and mental anguish, we received medical testimony that Mr. Fisher has suffered and continues to suffer from a form of a post traumatic stress disorder. Unquestionably claimant is entitled to be compensated for such damages, how-

ever, based on the record evidence and our observation of him during trial, we do not believe that Mr. Fisher's "disorder" is as severe as portrayed by his psychiatric expert. As noted, since his parole in 1944 claimant has been steadily employed and there was no showing his ability to work was impaired by any substantial psychological sequelae of his conviction and imprisonment. It should also be mentioned at this point that Mr. Fisher neither sought nor received any professional treatment for his alleged "chronic disorder" until several months before the subject trial. Given the circumstances, claimant has seemingly led a relatively well-adjusted life since his imprisonment and parole.

Having said this, however, we cannot forget nor should we lose sight of the loss of liberty and other circumstances of Mr. Fisher's imprisonment and parole. He was confined to a six-by-nine foot cell for 16 hours a day over a period of eleven years and had only minimal contact with his then wife and daughter. His letters were censored and no telephone calls were permitted. After being paroled in 1944, claimant was under strict supervision and significantly restricted in his activities (e.g., he had a nightly curfew and could not leave New York City without permission). During these 25 years Mr. Fisher was totally consumed with the reality that all this deprivation was the result of error and misconduct, and he was single-minded in his efforts to get his conviction overturned. As observed, this was achieved in 1958. The loss of freedom to say the least is painful to any person. That pain is all the more galling when accompanied by the realization that it was precipitated by the misconduct of a public official to whom society had entrusted the fair and just enforcement of our laws. In a country and state founded on personal liberty, it is certainly moral and proper to recognize and reaffirm the value of freedom. When one of our citizens is unjustly denied that freedom, he should be compensated as justice and equity direct. William Fisher lost substantially all his liberty and civil rights for 11 years and had them limited for 14 more. It is for this most of all that he is entitled to damages.

Therefore, considering all of the foregoing and the entire trial record, it is this court's determination that William Fisher be awarded the sum of $750,000 for all damages.

7

Barratry, Champerty, and Maintenance

7.1 BARRATRY

Barratry was defined by *Blackstone Commentaries* (1765) as "the offense of frequently exciting and stirring up suits and quarrels between his majesty's subjects." The prohibition against barratry probably developed as part of the Christian belief in medieval Europe that litigation was evil per se and that forgiveness of debtors was a fundamental virtue. (See 24 *California Law Review* 48, 1935.) Barratry should be distinguished from the offense of champerty, which is the act of supporting the litigation of another with the expectation of receiving part of the proceeds if the suit is successful; also distinguishable from barratry is the offense of maintenance, which is the act of supporting or promoting the litigation of another. (See § 7.2 herein.) Obviously, the original reasons for proscribing barratry, champerty, and maintenance are all now largely obsolete. However, there are barratry statutes in the various jurisdictions, as illustrated by Tennessee Code Ann. Sections 39–3405 to 39–3410. Section 39–3405 defines barratry in these terms:

(a) "Barratry" is the offense of stirring up litigation.

(b) A "barrator" is an individual, partnership, association or corporation who or which stirs up litigation.

(c) "Stirring up litigation" means instigating or attempting to instigate a person or persons to institute a suit at law or equity.

(d) "Instigating" means bringing it about that all or part of the expenses of the litigation are paid by the barrator or by a person or persons (other than the plaintiffs) acting in concert with the barrator, unless the instigation is justified.

> (e) "Justified" means that the instigator is related by blood or marriage to the plaintiff whom he instigates, or that the instigator is entitled by law to share with the plaintiff in money or property that is the subject of the litigation or that the instigator has a direct interest in the subject matter of the litigation or occupies a position of trust in relation to the plaintiff; or that the instigator is acting on behalf of a duly constituted legal aid society established by the Bar Association of Tennessee or any local bar association of this state which offers advice or assistance in all kinds of legal matters to all members of the public who come to it for advice or assistance and are unable because of poverty to pay legal fees.
>
> (f) "Direct interest" means a personal right or pecuniary right or liability.

Under the Tennessee statute the penalty for barratry is set forth under Section 39–3407:

> It shall be unlawful to engage in barratry. A person found guilty of barratry, if an individual, shall be guilty of a misdemeanor, and may be punished as provided by law; and if a corporation, may be fined not more than ten thousand dollars ($10,000). If the corporation be a foreign corporation, its certificate of authority to transact business in Tennessee shall be revoked by the district attorney general of the district in which the offense is committed.

The attorney who is found guilty of barratry, after a hearing, shall under Section 39–3410 be permanently or temporarily deprived of the "right to practice his profession, or a censure or reprimand, according to the gravity of the offense."

The above Tennessee statute on barratry was found by the federal district court in Tennessee in ACLU v. Tennessee (496 F. Supp 218, 1980) to be void, in that it impinged upon plaintiff's First Amendment right to associate for the purpose of gaining meaningful access to the courts. Here a non-profit corporation, Save Our Cumberland Mountains, Inc., and the American Civil Liberties Union, or ACLU, had filed suit to determine the constitutionality of the statute under 42 U.S. Code Section 1983. Closely analogous to the Tennessee statute was the barratry statute of Virginia, which the U.S. Supreme Court in 1963 found to be unconstitutional (NAACP v. Button, 371 US 415). The Virginia statute also imposed criminal penalties for solicitation of legal business or the acceptance of compensation from any person or organization not a party to a judicial proceeding and having no pecuniary interest in the litigation. The Virginia Supreme Court of Appeals had found the National Association for the Advancement of Colored People (NAACP) to have violated the barratry statute by holding meetings to inform black citizens of their legal rights in civil rights matters and by identifying prospective litigants and offering them the free help of an NAACP attorney to prosecute their civil rights claims. These activities, prohibited by the Virginia statute, were deemed by the highest court to be modes of association guaranteed and protected by the First Amendment. But the U.S. Supreme Court did not preclude a valid barratry statute when it is narrowly drawn so as not to offend the First Amendment, because the state does have a legitimate interest in regulating barratry so as to insure high professional standards for attorneys (In Re Primus, 436 US 412, 1978), and in preventing lay persons from engaging in the unauthorized practice of law. State interests might encompass protecting the recipient of free litigation from pressure to litigate or from fraudulent or deceptive activities. See generally 11 *Memphis State University Law Review* 426 (1981).

In recent days barratry has been associated with advertising and solicitation of legal business by attorneys in that such activities could have the motive of stirring up litigation. But the courts have not accepted that ploy, except to point out that "advertising that is false, deceptive or misleading is subject to restraint" (Bates v. State Bar of Arizona, 433 US 350, 1977). States may indeed regulate "in person" solicitation by attorneys for pecuniary gain, as shown in Ohralik v. Ohio State Bar Assn. (436 US 447, 1978), but only within narrow confines that do not infringe upon First Amendment rights. The state of Wisconsin, for example, regulates the professional conduct of attorneys to see that strife and litigation are not stirred up (Wis State Ann, Section 757.296), and the state of Montana takes the position of regulating public servants to see that there is no official misconduct such as performing an act in excess of lawful authority in order to obtain personal advantages (Mont Rev Code Ann, Section 45–7–401).

Barratry, according to the U.S. Supreme Court in NAACP v. Button (supra), was particularly objectionable in the presence of "malicious intent," which was "the essence of the common law offense of fomenting or stirring up litigation."

7.2 CHAMPERTY AND MAINTENANCE

The other two medieval concepts of champerty and maintenance were similar to barratry with respect to supporting or promoting litigation or committing frivolous act or acts. Champerty involved the additional element of providing the supporter of the litigation with an economic expectation if the litigation were successful, as illustrated in Draper v. Zebec (37 NE2d 952, Ind, 1941). Maintenance was simply the offense of supporting or promoting the litigation of another, as shown in Markarian v. Bartis (199 A 573, NH 1938). Champerty is defined in *Black's Law Dictionary* as

> [a] bargain by a stranger with a party to a suit, by which such third person undertakes to carry on the litigation at his own cost and risk, in consideration of receiving, if successful, a part of the proceeds or subject sought to be recovered.

The Code of Professional Responsibility of the American Bar Association, DR 5–103(b), delineated at §10.7 herein, without identifying the offense of champerty, provides:

While representing a client in connection with contemplated or pending litigation, a lawyer shall not advance or guarantee financial assistance to his client, except that a lawyer may advance or guarantee the expenses of litigation, including court costs, expenses of investigation, expenses of medical examination, and costs of obtaining and presenting evidence, provided the client remains ultimately liable for such expenses.

But the Model Rules of Professional Conduct, adopted by the American Bar Association in 1983, in Rule 1.9 (e) (1), state that a lawyer is permitted to advance expenses with the client's obligation no longer absolute but only contingent upon the success of the lawsuit. Thus, the contingent fee system, implicit in a plaintiff's mode of operation, was accepted, if not sanctioned, except in criminal cases, according to EC2–20 of the Code of Professional Responsibility.

Champerty statutes today in the various states are very limited in scope, as illustrated by Tennessee Code Ann. Sections 64–406 to 64–410, which pertain only to conveyances of land, to wit: an owner of land having title cannot convey unless he also has possession of the land. In England by the beginning of the fifteenth century, champerty was recognized as a criminal act, although certain civil remedies were provided for it including damages and avoidance of the champertous transfer of land. (See 13 *Memphis State University Law Review* 146, 1983.) Champerty was then defined as the voluntary giving or taking an interest in land in litigation or in land not in litigation, if the purpose was to rely upon judicial process to keep possession. Early English statutes were designed to thwart a wrongful possessor of land from obtaining clear and unfettered title to the land.

In modern England the issue of maintenance was raised in the 1980 decision of the English Court of Appeal in Trendtex Trading Corporation v. Credit Suisse (1980, 3 W.L.R. 367). Here the purchase and resale of cement to Nigeria was financed by Credit Suisse, the defendant and a creditor of the plaintiff. When the Central Bank of Nigeria refused to honor the letters of credit opened in favor of the plaintiff for the payment of the cement, the defendant undertook to finance the proceedings against the Central Bank of Nigeria in the English courts in consideration of the assignment of the claim of the plaintiff against the Central Bank of Nigeria. The plaintiff then successfully sued the Central Bank of Nigeria for the equivalent of $14 million, and the English Court of Appeal in 1977 rejected the defense of sovereign immunity. That case was on appeal one year later in 1978 when an agreement was made in Switzerland between plaintiff and defendant, reciting that an offer had been received from a third party to buy plaintiff's rights against the Central Bank of Nigeria, which rights had been assigned to defendant in 1976; the 1978 agreement also confirmed the fact that defendant agreed to pay plaintiff the equivalent of $800,000, which sum was sufficient to pay all the creditors of the plaintiff. A lawyer acting for the defendant then received 90 percent of the shares of stock of the plaintiff. Four days later defendant assigned the same rights of action to a third party for $1.1 million, making a quick profit of $300,000. In February 1978 defendant's lawyer journeyed to Nigeria and settled with the Central Bank of Nigeria for $8 million, and thus the unidentified third party on the second assignment of the right of action made an incredible profit of $6.9 million. Plaintiff's suit against the defendant in the English court argued that the second assignment of a bare right of action was illegal and void on the ground that it constituted maintenance, i.e., "improperly stirring up litigation and strife by giving aid to one party to bring or defend a claim without just cause or excuse." The English Court of Appeal held that, since defendant had financed the action in England, it had a legitimate, genuine, and sufficient interest in the suit, and therefore the assignment of the cause of action to the defendant did not constitute maintenance. It might be pointed out that, although the crime and tort of maintenance had been abolished by the English Criminal Law Act of 1967, a contract tainted by maintenance or champerty still contravened public policy and should be unenforceable in English courts. The second assignment to the unidentified third party would appear to have been champertous, since the third party bought the assignment as a marketable commodity only; what the English Court of Appeal had done was to sanction the trading of the cause of action like a transferable security or stock in the world market. See *Journal of Business Law* 3–5 (January 1981).

On August 21, 1986 in Puerto Rican Organization to Motivate, Enlighten and Serve Addicts (Promesa) v. City of New York, the federal district court for the Southern District of New York refused to award the plaintiff legal fees of almost $92,000 after the plaintiff had successfully settled a claim for $140,000 against the City for about $74,000. The court pointed out that the plaintiff "had no right to a hearing under its contract, never disputed the City's right to recover the money without a hearing and never discussed or resolved any right to a hearing," and therefore "should not be entitled to recover attorneys' fees merely because it put such a claim in its complaint." The point is that the attorneys' actions were frivolous and even champertous.

8

The Countersuit or Retaliatory Action

8.1 THE NEED FOR A COUNTER ACTION

As long as unwarranted and unjustifiable lawsuits are permitted to be filed by injury-conscious plaintiffs and by their avid attorneys, there can be no limit to the disheartening exorbitant costs and the time-consuming complexities of liability litigation today. Given a personal injury or property damage or economic loss, and an event which can in any manner whatsoever be remotely connected with or attributed to a given product or a given actor, or given act, these eager plaintiffs and their attorneys commence suit with little or no prior investigation of the claim. In essence, these ''hungry'' men and women argue that the facts will take care of themselves. And, furthermore, it is up to the judge or jury to decide whether there is, in fact, a valid cause of action permitting compensation. Such an undisciplined approach to liability is comparable to that of applauding the ''mystery train,'' i.e., while the train is apparently on a track, no one knows where or when it will stop, nor whom it will discharge, nor whom it will invite aboard, nor even the price of the ride. What is certain, however, is that the railroad will be sued for whatever happens. Courts and juries (as well as defendants' attorneys) have pondered over the problem of the ''mystery train,'' and only recently has a realistic counteraction been placed in the hands of defendants to compel these plaintiffs and their attorneys to stand up and be counted. It is the countersuit or the counterclaim or the retaliatory action to the malpractice action and the liability lawsuit that gives hope to bringing about some control over the frivolous lawsuit and the frivolous defense.

But the tremendous increase in the number of malpractice suits in recent years is not entirely due to frivolous lawsuits. There is admittedly a general proliferation of civil litigation resulting from the premise that the U.S. citizen bonafidedly believes that he or she is entitled to be compensated for any hurt, inconvenience, distraction, or indeed any injury, disease, death, or economic loss which can be attributed by any stretch of the imagination to another person, entity, or thing! (See Warren Freedman, *Products Liability for Corporate Counsels, Controllers and Product Safety Executives*, Van Nostrand Reinhold, 1984.) Other reasons include, for medical malpractice actions, the increased public use of health services and the utilization of more sophisticated medical procedures and technology. Probably of equal importance in the medical malpractice crisis is the breakdown of the traditional personal relationship between a doctor and his patient. (See generally 75 *Marquette Law Review* 93, 1981.)

In the medical malpractice field, the authors Page Keeton and Robert E. Keeton, in *Cases and Materials on the Laws of Torts* (West Publishing Co., 1977), at page 1126 opined:

> Often, the mere filing of a medical malpractice claim against a physician engenders a significant amount of harm to his reputation, and under current insurance practices brings about a substantial increase in his insurance costs. During the past year or so, a number of countersuits have been filed by physicians against lawyers who represent patients with claims which prove unmeritorious. As of this time (June 1977), it does not appear that these efforts have met with any success on any theory.

Indeed, the number of successful countersuits filed by physicians has greatly increased during the past ten years, but the number of successful actions remains pitifully low and almost insignificant. The physician who is frivolously sued by a patient who should have known that the named defendant physician had never treated the patient should be entitled to compensatory and perhaps punitive or exemplary damages. A doctor's reputation clearly suffers when a malpractice action is brought against him; today ''malpractice'' is an ill-famed word, almost synonymous with quackery or charlatanism (see 9 *Western Reserve Law Review* 471, 1958). Under Section 587, Comment c, of Restatement (Second) of Torts the plaintiff in the malpractice suit enjoys immunity to publish false and defamatory material about the defendant physician so long as the plaintiff stays within the bounds of the lawsuit. However, the threat of a doctor counterattacking with a suit for abuse of process, malicious prosecution, or similar action may cause a disgruntled patient and his lawyer to reconsider before bringing a frivolous suit.

8.2 OTHER THEORIES AND OTHER REMEDIES

Liability for frivolous lawsuits and frivolous defenses has been predicated upon abuse of process (Chapter 3 herein), malicious prosecution (Chapter 4 herein), wrongful civil proceedings (Chapter 5 herein), and false arrest or false imprisonment (Chapter 6 herein). In addition to these theories of liability and remedies there are actions for barratry, defamation, invasion of privacy, negligence, prima facie tort, unprofessional conduct, and willful infliction of emotional distress.

Barratry is the offense of "frequently exciting and stirring up quarrels and lawsuits," as delineated in Lyddon v. Shaw (372 NE2d 685, Ill, 1972), but courts have promptly dismissed barratry claims by stating that it is the general practice and not the particular, singular act that defines barratry. Section 158 of the California Penal Code defines barratry as "the practice of exciting groundless judicial proceedings," and under Section 159 the punishment is that of a misdemeanor, but conviction under the statute requires that the defendant institute at least three proceedings with "corrupt or malicious intent to vex or annoy." Furthermore, it has been held in Moiel v. Sandlin (571 SW2d 567, Tex, 1978) that the offense of barratry in Texas is a public remedy and is not available as a private remedy. It has been pointed out in 19 *Washburn Law Journal* (1980) at page 461 that the barratry offense can also adversely affect the physicians themselves as exemplified by the established "countersuit funds" to aid physicians in their malpractice lawsuits: "Barratry charges may be filed against contributors under a statute prohibiting 'stirring up' and 'encouraging litigation.' "

Defamation is the invasion of one's interest in reputation and good name, and involves a communication to a third person which adversely affects the opinions of persons in the community of the person defamed. Attorneys, physicians, and other professionals have endeavored without much success to use the defamation theory or remedy against the frivolous lawsuit. The underlying fact is that nearly all jurisdictions grant an absolute privilege to statements made in a judicial proceeding (Umansky v. Urquhart, 84 Cal App3d 368, 1978). As long as the defamatory statements are in some manner relevant and material to the judicial proceeding, the action for libel or slander will not succeed. Such defenses to defamation as consent, truth, and other privileges are also applicable, but in Jankelson v. Cisel (3 Wash App 139, 1970) a dentist was successful in a countersuit against a former patient who made slanderous and libelous statements to other dentists about the plaintiff dentist and also communicated the defamatory utterances to the dental society concerning the alleged malpractice; the successful dentist was awarded damages and a permanent injunction. There is also the success of physicians in Peerman v. Sidicane (605 SW2d 242, Tenn, 1980) and in Raine v. Drasin (621 SW2d 895, Ky, 1981), the latter case bringing the two doctors each $10,000 in compensatory damages for humiliation, mortification, and loss of reputation.

Invasion of privacy was the approach taken in Wolfe v. Arroyo (543 SW2d 11, Tex, 1976), but the Texas court held that communications in a judicial proceeding are absolutely privileged and therefore inadmissible in an action for invasion of privacy. The cause of action might describe an intrusion upon the professional's solitude or seclusion, or public disclosure of private facts, or placing the professional in a false light publicly, but it would appear that little or no success has been achieved in this route of invasion of privacy (Tappen v. Ager, 599 F2d 376, 10th Cir, 1979).

Negligence is another theory or remedy in the countersuit, particularly attorney professional negligence, which attempts to find the attorney culpable in bringing the original malpractice action. In practice it appears that there are two bases for these allegations of negligence, to wit: breach of duty owed by the attorney to a third person to exercise reasonable care, and violation by the attorney of the Code of Professional Responsibility of the American Bar Association inhibiting attorneys from bringing frivolous lawsuits or answering frivolously. (See §10.7 herein.) But courts have consistently rejected the view that an attorney has a duty of care to third persons or parties (Bickel v. Mackie, 447 F Supp 1376, Iowa, 1976). At most, the attorney's duty of care is owed to his own client and to the legal system as a whole, but breach of such duty cannot be the basis for a third person or third party bringing suit in negligence against the attorney (Berlin v. Nathan, 381 NE2d 1367, Ill, 1978). The underlying policy reason is that, if an attorney is held liable for negligence in bringing a frivolous case, his efficacy as an advocate and his value to the court will be tarnished because an attorney would then not accept the problem case in the first instance. The question of privity between an attorney and the adverse party was discussed in the California case of Norton v. Hines (49 Cal App3d 917, 1975), but the court wound up on an "intended third party beneficiary theory": "In the case at bar a former litigant is suing adverse counsel. Clearly an adverse party is not an intended beneficiary of the adverse counsel's client." The second base for the negligence cause of action is violation by the attorney of the Code of Professional Responsibility and similar professional standards (see § 4.5 herein). But courts have clearly rejected such claims in negligence on the ground that the Code of Professional Responsibility can furnish no basis for a private cause of action (Brody v. Ruby, 267 NW2d 902, Iowa, 1978).

The prima facie tort is defined as "the infliction of intentional harm, resulting in damage, without excuse of justification, by an act or series of acts which would otherwise be lawful," as illustrated in Belsky v. Lowenthal, 405 NYS2d 62, 1978). But in the countersuit context plaintiffs have achieved little success: "This rationale should not be an occasion for setting aside large bodies of case law which have defined our limits, established our guidelines, and set forth the essential elements of traditional tort" (Belsky v. Lowenthal, supra). The New York Court of Appeals in its 1978 decision in Drago v. Buonagurio (386 NE2d 821) refused to accept the prima facie tort in another medical malpractice countersuit.

Unprofessional conduct embraces any behavior or conduct which the plaintiff may cite, but courts are reluctant to predicate liability upon breach of such codes or styles of behavior (Martin v. Trevino, 578 SW2d 763, Tex, 1978).

Willful infliction of emotional distress is another theory or remedy that has met with no success, primarily because of the prerequisite of outrageous conduct and necessary proof of "willful infliction." See Section 46 of Restatement (Second) of Torts, and note Joseph v. Markovitz (551 P2d 571, Ariz, 1976).

8.3 SUCCESSFUL COUNTERSUITS BY PHYSICIANS IN MALPRACTICE MATTERS

A chronological survey of successful countersuits by physicians in malpractice matters might include the following cases:

Berlin v. Nathan (381 NE2d 1367, Ill, 1978). Here the radiologist, an orthopedic surgeon, and a hospital were named as defendants in the malpractice suit brought by a female tennis enthusiast and her husband, who sought $250,000 in damages on two causes of action because *all* of the defendants had, on October 1, 1973, allegedly failed to discover a fracture in her right fifth (tennis) finger and an embedded bone chip, and, as a result thereof, the finger had become permanently disabled. Specifically, the radiologist was charged with negligence in (1) failing to x-ray all necessary views of the injured finger; (2) failing to diagnose a fracture in the x-rays that were taken; (3) wrongfully diagnosing a dislocation causing plaintiff to sustain improper treatment; and (4) failing to let the x-rays dry long enough to obtain a clear and precise picture before reading them and before diagnosing the plaintiff's condition.

For reasons that are perfectly obvious the plaintiffs withdrew their suit *immediately* prior to trial. Evidently the defendant orthopedic surgeon and defendant hospital were pleased that the lawsuit was terminated. But, since the radiologist had carefully reviewed the x-rays and was convinced that there had been no fracture whatsoever, he promptly sued, not only the plaintiff and her husband, but their two attorneys, contending that all four persons were "guilty" of breaching "a duty" (owed to the plaintiff-radiologist) to refrain from willfully and wantonly bringing suit against him and involving him in litigation without having reasonable cause to believe that he had been guilty of malpractice that proximately caused "injury" to the female patient. Furthermore, the defendant-husband of the patient "willfully and wantonly incited and caused his wife to file the aforesaid malpractice suit solely in retribution for real or imagined discourtesies to his family" by the orthopedic surgeon. The plaintiff-radiologist alleged that the two attorneys for the plaintiffs "brought suit against the plaintiff willfully and wantonly and without reasonable cause," in that (1) "at no time before filing suit did these attorneys submit the aforesaid x-rays which were at all times available to any physician" of the patient "to a duly licensed physician specializing in radiology for an opinion as to whether the appropriate views had been taken or the films were of good quality or the films had been correctly read and interpreted"; (2) "at no time before filing suit did they, in fact, obtain an opinion from any duly licensed physician that the aforesaid x-rays did not include the appropriate number and types of views or were of poor quality or had been incorrectly read and interpreted"; (3) "at no time before filing suit did they obtain or secure an opinion from any duly licensed physician that any condition which presently existed regarding the little finger of the right hand'' of the patient ''proximately resulted from the malpractice of either'' the radiologist or the orthopedic surgeon; (4) ''as of the date'' they ''were consulted and/or retained'' by the patient ''the running of the statute of limitations with respect to the malpractice action'' against the radiologist was not imminent, and sufficient time remained for them to perform a reasonable investigation of the claim; (5) ''they knew or should have known that the allegations . . . were totally without justification in that . . . all possible views [of the injury were in fact taken, i.e., an oblique, a lateral], and A.P., a fracture was diagnosed; a dislocation was correctly diagnosed and that said dislocation constitutes the principal injury sustained by virtue of the tennis accident, and the antiquated method by which x-rays 'dry' was not in effect at Skokie Valley Community Hospital and therefore said charges were totally inapplicable''; and (6) ''they specified an ad damnum in a malpractice suit against the plaintiff . . . which bore no reasonable relationship to the injuries allegedly sustained . . . said ad damnum was devised in order to frighten and intimidate the said plaintiff which may adversely affect his ability to procure malpractice insurance at reasonable rates.''

In essence, the radiologist alleged that the two attorneys were negligent in performing their duties as attorneys in not investigating the malpractice suit before filing it. The patient's husband (also a lawyer) was alleged to have violated the Illinois barratry statute which statute required suspension from the practice of law up to six months if a person ''shall wickedly and willfully excite and stir up any suits or quarrels between the people of the state, either at law or otherwise, with a view to prompt strife and contention.''

The jury verdict for the radiologist was $2,000 in compensatory damages and $6,000 in punitive damages, as of June 1, 1978. Clearly the malpractice suit was unnecessary litigation, at least with respect to the defendant radiologist, and his recovery of $8,000 in damages is convincing evidence that plaintiffs and their two attorneys had simply not investigated her specious claim against him. The compensation awarded the radiologist was but small satisfaction for the indignity and expenditure of time and money which he suffered. It took patience and fortitude on the part of the radiologist not to accept the discontinuance of the suit and to pursue his own remedy subsequently.

Canty v. Moore and Eck (decided by the Montana Supreme Court in 1976). Here the Montana action resulted in a judgment against defendant-patient Ida Moore of $9,700 in special damages, $50,000 in general damages, and $50,000 in punitive damages, for a total of $109,000, plus costs, in favor of Dr. Charles R. Canty, an orthopedic surgeon practicing in Butte, Montana. (Actually Ida Moore ''took'' a default judgment, and then entered into a compromise settlement with Dr. Canty.) Interestingly, Ida Moore had initially sought the opinion of three attorneys before suing Dr. Canty; only defendant attorney Eck advised her that she had a cause of action against Dr. Canty. Ida Moore "completely disregarded" the advice of the three attorneys and filed suit against Dr. Canty. Her testimony at the subsequent trial, according to District Judge James Freebourn, "not only did not support any cause of action" against Dr. Canty, but "in effect, supported the position taken by Dr. Charles R. Canty." Judge Freebourn found that Ida Moore "was actuated by malice against the plaintiff in this action, and there was a total absence of probable cause for continuing the lawsuit." The court found that as a result of Ida Moore's suit against Dr. Canty, he was "prevented from pursuing his active practice as an orthopedic surgeon"; that Dr. Canty suffered "humiliation, adverse publicity, embarrassment, mental distress, anxiety and concern." Judge Freebourn concluded that the "continued prosecution" of the malpractice action against Dr. Canty was "totally unjustified and represented willful and wanton misconduct on the part of Ida Moore."

According to the complaint, defendant attorney Eck on January 30, 1975, had filed a malpractice suit against Dr. Canty. He and the plaintiff had filed certain answers to interrogatories wherein they represented that certain physicians would support the allegations of negligence against Dr. Canty, but in truth and in fact, "none of the physicians named in response to the interrogatories had agreed to testify for defendant Moore; in fact at the time the interrogatories were answered the defendant attorney Eck had not even conferred with the doctors. . . . " Another issue delineated in the complaint revolved about a signature on the operative consent form; it was alleged that Attorney Eck had agreed that, if the signature was that of Mrs. Moore and not of Dr. Canty, Attorney Eck would withdraw as counsel and the case would be dismissed. But, despite proof that the signature was Mrs. Moore's, Attorney Eck did not withdraw nor dismiss the suit. Apparently at the trial of the malpractice action against Dr. Canty and the hospital on April 13, 1976, defendant attorney Eck and defendant Ida Moore filed a motion to continue with an affidavit describing an alleged "conspiracy" with hospital personnel and other physicians against Mrs. Moore. Although the motion to continue was denied, defendant attorney Eck during the eleven days of trial was unable to prove that the hospital records were incomplete or inaccurate. Indeed, at the trial Attorney Eck advised the court that he did not have an expert witness to support any of the allegations. On motion by Dr. Canty for a directed verdict, the motion was granted and the case was dismissed.

It should be noted that in the malpractice suit Dr. Canty was but one of the two original defendants, the other defendant being St. James Community Hospital. Apparently Ida Moore on February 9, 1972, had entered the hospital as a patient complaining of back pains. She alleged that she sustained burns about her body due to a defective heating pad, and required surgical treatment. It seems that Dr. Canty on or about February 14, 1972, had advised Ida Moore to undergo a myelogram at the hospital, which she did and also suffered injuries. (Note that Dr. Canty was not her attending physician.) Ida Moore had apparently signed a consent to the myelogram but then subsequently argued that she did not recall the signing nor was the signature hers.

Lee v. Hudson and Willard (decided by the federal court in Georgia in 1979). In August 1976 plaintiff oral surgeon was sued for a 1974 malpractice by his patient Ray Wright together with the Veterans Administration as co-plaintiff; the malpractice action was brought in the U.S. District Court, Northern District of Georgia, Rome Division. The causes of action included a charge of assault and battery by Dr. Lee. Four months later, Federal Judge Henderson granted a partial summary judgment in favor of Dr. Lee. Shortly thereafter, Ray Wright and his two attorneys voluntarily dismissed the complaint against Dr. Lee.

The filing of a countersuit by Dr. Lee against his patient and the two attorneys for malicious prosecution prompted defendants Wright, Hudson, and Willard to accept a consent judgment against themselves in January 1979. The terms of settlement included a $10,000 judgment ''without interest for the first fifteen days'' in favor of Dr. Lee against the three defendants. Also, the two attorneys were required to place a public ad in the local newspaper apologizing to Dr. Lee for their having failed to investigate the malpractice claim before filing suit against Dr. Lee. The public apology included the statement that ''Dr. Lee had done nothing wrong and should not have been subjected to the above described lawsuit.''

It should be noted that Dr. Lee's medical malpractice insurance policy had been cancelled as a result of the filing of this frivolous malpractice suit against him. The joining of the Veterans Administration as co-plaintiff in the original malpractice suit against Dr. Lee was deemed by Dr. Lee to be ''malicious'' because by ''adding believably (?) and credence to the lawsuit which the defendants knew or should have known had no basis in law or fact,'' Dr. Lee was ''severely embarrassed in front of his colleagues and family.''

Drago v. Buonagurio (391 NYS2d 61, 1977; rev 402 NYS2d 250, 1978; rev 413 NYS2d 910, 1979).* The complaint alleged that the plaintiff, a doctor, and others, had been sued in a malpractice action brought by defendant Madeline Buonagurio, as administratrix of the estate of Francis Buonagurio, deceased, wherein it was alleged that because of certain specified acts of malpractice committed by the plaintiff physician, Francis Buonagurio had died and his estate sustained damage in the sum of $1.5 million. That malpractice action was commenced at the direction of the defendant attorney Brownstein. But the fact of the matter was that (1) the plaintiff physician never had Francis Buonagurio as a patient during the illness which allegedly caused his death, and (2) plaintiff did not treat him directly or indirectly during said illness. Indeed, no

*In December 1978 the decision was again reversed, as the New York Court of Appeals (402 NYS2d 250, 386 NE2d 821, 1978) ruled that the complaint failed to state a cause of action in negligence, in abuse of process, in malicious prosecution, as well as for a ''prima facie tort'' of intentional malicious injury to another by otherwise lawful means without economic or social justification, but solely to harm the other.

basis existed for designating plaintiff as a defendant in the malpractice action: it was done indiscriminately and purely as a discovery device in order to ascertain where responsibility could be placed. The complaint alleged that defendant lawyer Brownstein's actions were malicious, unethical, and grossly negligent, and that the unwarranted suit caused plaintiff physician to suffer mental anguish and defamation of character. On these facts, Special Term of the New York Supreme Court for Schenectady County, on February 2, 1977, decided that the complaint failed to state facts sufficient to constitute a cause of action against the lawyer and the suing patient's estate, and so the complaint was dismissed. However, the New York Appellate Division, 3rd Dept., reversed and accepted the physician's contention that the lawyer and client had sued him frivolously and "discriminately," not in expectation of establishing any liability on his part, but solely "as a discovery device in order to ascertain where responsibility could be placed." A prima facie tort had occurred, according to the court, where damage-causing harm (i.e., mental anguish and damage to reputation) is intentionally inflicted without justification.

The New York appellate court initially reviewed the "various possible tort causes of action" and found that, while the facts herein "contain many of the elements common to traditional theories of torts, they do not fit neatly into any of them." The court inquired:

> Must we conclude, therefore, that since the traditional theories of tort do not appear to afford relief to plaintiff, he has no remedy? We think not, for the law should never suffer an injury and a damage without a remedy.

Thereupon the court looked to the "more innovative theory (which is) designated prima facie tort," as first enunciated by Mr. Justice Oliver Wendell Holmes in Aikens v. Wisconsin (195 US 194, 1904). Citing several New York cases recognizing the prima facie tort, Judge Sweeney of the New York Appellate Division spelled out the tort as "the intentional infliction of harm, resulting in damage, without excuse or justification, by an act or series of acts which would otherwise be lawful and which (act or series of) acts do not fall within the categories of traditional tort." The court found that the acts of the defendant lawyer and the estate of the suing patient were "not only intentional and wrongful, but, under the unusual circumstances alleged, (were) irresponsible and without justification." The court concluded:

> The fact that a cause of action is new, novel or nameless should not deprive an injured person of a remedy. The law of torts is not static. The reported cases clearly demonstrate that new and nameless torts are being recognized constantly to cope with society's economic, social and technological changes (*Prosser, Torts* (4th ed.), p. 3.). The progress of the common law is marked by many cases of first impression. The instant case has its genesis in the drastic increase in the number of medical malpractice actions during recent years, many of which are considered baseless by members of the medical profession.

In finding the commission of the prima facie tort of intentional infliction of harm the New York Appellate Division issued a caveat: "Upholding the sufficiency of this complaint does not mean that plaintiff will ultimately succeed on the trial of his allegations, nor should this opinion be read as creating or recognizing a distinctly new cause of action whenever a physician escapes malpractice liability and claims he was wrongfully charged in the first place."

Peerman v. Sidicane (605 SW2d 242, Tenn, 1980). A female patient had an attorney file a complaint against her treating physician alleging that the physician had negligently diagnosed gonorrhea and had delayed tests necessary to her treatment, in order to obtain "kickbacks" from a medical laboratory. The trial court granted summary judgment in favor of the physician, who then countersued the patient and her attorney. The evidence revealed that the physician had informed the patient that she might have gonorrhea after her examination, but treated her for acute pelvic inflammation until recommended tests results were received. Seven days later he informed the patient that the culture for gonorrhea was negative. Patient's attorney made no investigation, took no depositions, and interviewed no physicians as to the appropriate standard of care. Her attorney had no information about the alleged kickback scheme, but conjured up the issue.

The jury awarded the physician $3,000 compensatory and $8,500 punitive damages against the attorney, but dismissed the claim against the patient. The Tennessee Court of Appeals affirmed, pointing out that the attorney had continued to press the case without his client's consent and had entered allegations from pure speculation on his part. The malicious prosecution action was therefore upheld against the attorney only.

Raine v. Drasin (621 SW2d 895, Ky, 1981). A cardiac patient suffered damage to his shoulder while hospitalized, and upon release from the hospital he engaged an attorney to initiate a malpractice claim. The complaint prepared by the first attorney was signed by the second attorney because the first attorney had another hospital as a client and did not want his name on the complaint. An amended complaint, also signed by the second attorney, named a radiologist and an orthopedist as defendants. But some weeks later the plaintiff-patient agreed to dismiss these two physicians from the case, and they immediately sued for malicious prosecution.

The Kentucky jury returned verdicts against the attorneys, to wit: $37,500 compensatory and punitive damages against the first attorney, and $12,500 damages against the second attorney. The Kentucky Court of Appeals ruled that a statement imputing a general want of professional knowledge or skill to a physician is recognized to be defamatory per se, and therefore the physicians were entitled to recover for reputational damage. But the second attorney, who merely signed the pleadings, did not entertain any "malice" as required for a malicious prosecution action, and therefore the verdict against him was reversed. (The court also ordered a new trial on the issue of punitive damages.)

Shulman v. Miskell (626 F2d 173, DC, 1980). A patient filed suit against the physician for malpractice in 1977, and, although the trial court dismissed the punitive damage claim, it found in favor of the physician on the compensatory damage claim. The physician then filed an action for malicious prosecution in 1978, contending that the claim for punitive damages had been brought maliciously and without probable cause, and the trial court here dismissed that claim under the one-year statute of limitations. The District of Columbia Court of Appeals reversed, holding that this trial court had erred in computing the time period; the limitations period began when the prior malpractice suit was terminated in favor of the physician, not when it was commenced. Therefore, the suit for punitive damages here was timely filed.

Nelson v. Miller (607 P2d 438, Kan, 1980). A physician was one of several physicians named as defendants in a malpractice suit filed in 1976; the malpractice complaint alleged negligent treatment of a pregnant patient, to wit, without a prior examination for pregnancy, a dilation and curettage (D&C) was performed on her and the fetus was injured. More than a year later, in 1977, the malpractice action against the physician was dismissed without prejudice, and later the trial court granted summary judgment in favor of the remaining physicians. The physician then filed the countersuit against the patient's attorneys and the trial court dismissed his suit; but the Kansas Supreme Court reversed on the ground that the physician's complaint stated a cause of action for malicious prosecution because the prior legal proceeding was initiated without probable cause, the patient acted with malice, the earlier suit terminated in favor of the physician, and the physician suffered damages. But the attorneys for the patient were not liable for negligence to the physician, except in the malicious prosecution action.

8.4 UNSUCCESSFUL COUNTERSUITS BY PHYSICIANS IN MALPRACTICE MATTERS

A survey chronologically of unsuccessful countersuits by physicians in malpractice matters, representing the weight of authority in the United States today, might include the following cases:

Hoppenstein v. Zemek (62 AD2d 979, 1978). Herein a man had been brought to a hospital after an apparent fall down a flight of steps. He died ten hours later of cardio-respiratory failure triggered by cerebraledema. The patient's next of kin filed a wrongful death suit against the hospital and four physicians. After one day of trial the case was settled for $75,000, but only the hospital paid. One of the four physicians then sued the patient's next of kin and their attorneys, and charged that he was wrongfully joined as a defendant with the deliberate intent of forcing a settlement from his insurer or the hospital, and with the deliberate intent to use him as an expert witness without payment. The physician sued for abuse of process, malicious prosecution, and prima facie tort. After the trial court dismissed his complaint he appealed, only to have the New York Appellate Division, 2nd Dept., affirm. The physician's countersuit was dismissed on the ground that "the plaintiff doctor concededly did have some involvement in the treatment of the decedent." There was at least colorable validity to the joinder of the physician as a defendant in the wrongful death suit.

Bickel v. Mackie (447 F Supp 1376, Iowa, 1976). A countersuit by a physician against a patient and his attorney after the patient's malpractice suit was *summarily* dismissed. The plaintiff physician had alleged (1) malicious prosecution, (2) abuse of process, (3) negligent practice of law, (4) conspiracy to harm him, and (5) failure to comply with an attorney's Code of Professional Responsibility. On defendant's motion for judgment the federal court ruled that Iowa was one of seventeen states that required proof of "*special* injury," not merely harm to reputation, to support a claim for malicious prosecution. And, without proof of malice, a cause of action for abuse of process did not exist. On the issue of the lawyer's negligence in the practice of law, the court remarked that all that the attorney did was to advise the patient to commence the medical malpractice action. There was no basis under traditional tort remedies for the physician's countersuit.

Pantone v. Demos (375 NE2d 480, Ill, 1978). The countersuing plaintiffs unsuccessfully based their action upon willful and wanton filing of a civil lawsuit and upon professional negligence of an attorney. Here the patient entered a hospital to have a child, and was given a chest x-ray by a radiologist. Later another physician performed two venous cut downs on her. That same day she died of childbirth complications. The patient's husband sued the radiologist and the physician for wrongful death; upon a motion for summary judgment the complaints against both defendants were dismissed. Suit by the two physicians was then brought against the husband and his attorney, but the trial court dismissed their action. The Illinois appellate court affirmed upon the basis that public interest in free access to the courts outweighed the harm to the physicians who were improperly named in the medical malpractice action. The court also dismissed the claim against the attorney for malpractice because there was no duty owed to the physicians in the absence of an attorney-client relationship.

O'Toole v. Franklin (569 P2d 561, 1978). The Oregon Supreme Court upheld the lower court's dismissal of an action by two physicians against several attorneys. The action had been brought for malicious prosecution, and for negligence in practicing law because the attorneys did not inquire from the patient whether the physicians had been treating him at the time when the malpractice was alleged to have taken place. The highest Oregon court ruled that the "special injury requirement" had not been met by the two physicians; there was no "immediate interference with his person, property, income or credit," that the action was not maliciously instituted, and that the two physicians who were "uniquely vulnerable to being harmed thereby [did not go] beyond the ordinary hardships of similar cases."

Stopka v. Lesser (402 NE2d 781, Ill, 1980). A patient was treated badly at a hospital emergency room, and his attorney filed a malpractice suit against the hospital; five months later the attorney amended the complaint, adding an additional physician who was an inactive hospital staff member not involved with the patient's treatment. Seventeen months later this physician was dismissed from the case, and the resulting countersuit by this physician was based on malicious prosecution and legal malpractice. The Illinois appellate court affirmed the dismissal of the countersuit on the ground that the physician did not have a "special injury," i.e., an injury beyond the anxiety, loss of time, attorneys' fees and necessity for defending one's reputation, all of which are the necessary ingredients of most lawsuits. But the court implied that Illinois should reassess its requisite of "special damages":

> It should result in the establishment of an alternative that would impose a meaningful duty upon attorneys to ascertain whether the party sued is possibly liable for a wrong committed and, absent any exigency, where that possibility does not exist, to effectively deter meritless litigation by providing a recovery from the attorney to the victim without the requirement of special damages.

Ayyildiz v. Kidd (266 SE2d 108, Va, 1980). After the physician won a malpractice case brought by his patient, the physician filed a motion for judgment against the attorney for the patient, claiming that the attorney had prosecuted him unsuccessfully, with malice, and without probable cause. The Virginia Supreme Court affirmed the trial court's dismissal, holding that the malicious prosecution doctrine does not extend to a civil proceeding but only delineates criminal proceedings, unless there is an arrest of the plaintiff, seizure of property, or some other special injury to him. Furthermore, the attorney for the patient was under no legal duty to the physician.

Friedman v. Dozoroc (312 NW2d 585, Mich, 1981). Michigan also requires proof of "special injury" to support an action for malicious prosecution, and so the physician was unsuccessful in his countersuit against the attorneys who had represented the patient's family survivors in the malpractice action. Costs of legal defense, harm to reputation as a physician, increase in annual malpractice insurance premiums, and the loss of two young associates from the physician's office because they could no longer afford to pay the increased premiums, all did not satisfy the requisite "special injury" definition in Michigan.

Spencer v. Burglass (337 So2d 596, La App, 1976). Louisiana dismissed a surgeon's countersuit for failure to state a cause of action, reciting the contention that the original suit had violated a duty owed to the physicians as a result of the oath the attorney took upon admission to practice. Nor did the court accept the physician's claim that a duty was owed her under Canon 30 of the Canons of Professional Ethics entitled "Justifiable and Unjustifiable Litigation." Furthermore, the attorney's alleged failure to interview witnesses prior to trial did not constitute "malice" in the malicious prosecution cause of action:

We can construe this allegation to mean negligence or ineptitude on defendant's part in his trial preparation and perhaps, if this caused the loss of the case, this failure might provide a basis for an action in malpractice against him by his client, but we cannot construe the naked allegation to imply [that] the defendant's failure to interview his witnesses before trial constituted a reckless disregard as to whether his client's [not his] charge of malpractice against plaintiff was false or not. . . . At worst, the allegation is that the defendant went to trial with a poor case and got his just desserts [*sic*], to wit, he lost. If that constitutes malice, the courtrooms are full of malicious attorneys. This we cannot accept.

8.5 THE RETALIATORY ACTION

The retaliatory action was defined in Simon v. Satterlee & Stephens (decided by a New York Supreme Court on November 12, 1985, in these words: "[E]ach party alleges that the claims of the opposing party in a previous case [were] malicious and meritless. . . . " Here plaintiff's allegations related to defendants' misconduct in the discovery phase of a libel action, to wit: "Satterlee obtained an order to depose all of the defendants in the libel action but when a ruling was called for, Satterlee left the courthouse without taking the ordered depositions." Defendants in turn alleged that plaintiff had failed to appear at a deposition six months earlier, but appeared at a hearing before another justice and "sought a ruling prior to the taking of his deposition" that the directors of Seaboard Surety had not produced ordered documents. A subsequent court order found defendants "had evaded their duty to appear for the examination," and the document they sought had not been delivered "because those defendants had expanded their original document request." The New York Supreme Court, New York County, found that such actions did not constitute "abuse of process." The court reminded the parties: "The remedy for discovery disputes is a motion for contempt and sanctions . . . and not the commencement of a separate and collateral proceeding." The complaint was dismissed: "This type of spiraling escalation of law suits cannot be permitted as unnecessary and wasteful of judicial resources."

The Indiana Court of Appeals in Wong v. Taylor (422 NE2d 1279, 1981) spoke in terms of sending a disaster message to physicians who contemplated retaliatory legal action after the termination of the prior medical malpractice action. Protection of the attorney was uppermost in the court's mind in holding that an objective standard should govern the reasonableness of an attorney's action in instituting litigation for a client. The question is

whether the claim merits litigation against the defendant in question on the basis of the facts known to the attorney when the suit was commenced. The question is answered by determining that no competent and reasonable attorney familiar with the law of the forum would consider that the claim was worthy of litigation on the basis of the facts known by the attorney who instituted suit.

The question is admittedly pregnant with a negative answer because "an attorney may institute and present a case vigorously and in a manner as favorable to his client as the rules of law and professional ethics will permit" (Weaver v. Superior Court, 95 Cal App3d 166, 1979). The Indiana court concluded:

> While the tort [of malicious prosecution] assumes litigant responsibility, it was not created for, nor does it contemplate, the need for a remedy designed to deter attorneys from filing baseless lawsuits. The clear reluctance of the courts to find attorneys liable for malicious prosecution is evidence of the questioned efficacy of such an action in promoting this end.

8.6 PROCEDURAL ASPECTS OF THE COUNTERSUIT

Perhaps typical of the procedural requirements for the counterclaim is Section 3019 of the New York Civil Practice Law and Rules, which delineates "counterclaims" and "cross-claims" as follows:

> §3019. Counterclaims and cross-claims.
>
> (a) Subject of counterclaims. A counterclaim may be any cause of action in favor of one or more defendants or a person whom a defendant represents against one or more plaintiffs, a person whom a plaintiff represents or a plaintiff and other persons alleged to be liable.
>
> (b) Subject of cross-claims. A cross-claim may be any cause of action in favor of one or more defendants or a person whom a defendant represents against one or more defendants, a person whom a defendant represents or a defendant and other persons alleged to be liable. A cross-claim may include a claim that the party against whom it is asserted is or may be liable to the cross-claimant for all or part of a claim asserted in the action against the cross-claimant.
>
> (c) Counterclaim against trustee or nominal plaintiff. In an action brought by a trustee or in the name of a plaintiff who has no actual interest in the contract upon which it is founded, a claim against the plaintiff shall not be allowed as a counterclaim, but a claim existing against the person beneficially interested shall be allowed as a counterclaim to the extent of the plaintiff's claim, if it might have been so allowed in an action brought by the person beneficially interested.
>
> (d) Cause of action in counterclaim or cross-claim deemed in complaint. A cause of action contained in a counterclaim or a cross-claim shall be treated, as far as practicable, as if it were contained in a complaint, except that separate process, trial or judgment may not be had unless the court so orders. Where a person not a party is alleged to be liable he shall be served with a summons and a copy of the answer containing the counterclaim or cross-claim, whereupon he shall become a defendant and he shall serve a reply or answer as if he were originally a party.

The thrust of the statute was to eliminate all historical limitations on setoffs and recoupments (Getlan v. Hofstra University, 342 NYS2d, 44). In general, in a ''counterclaim,'' a cause of action is asserted by one or more plaintiffs and other persons alleged to be liable; on the other hand, the ''cross-claim'' is asserted against one or more co-defendants and others alleged to be liable. See Seligson v. Chase Manhattan Bank National Assn, (376 NYS2d 899, 1975). Neither the ''counterclaim'' nor the ''cross-claim'' need arise out of the same transaction, for the thrust of the practice is the economical resolution of interrelated lawsuits and interrelated claims.

Effective January 31, 1979, the state of Texas statutorily recognized the validity of a countersuit at least with respect to a health care liability claim. The statute is entitled the Medical Liability and Insurance Improvement Act, Article 4590 i of the Revised Civil Statutes of the State of Texas, Subchapter H, Bad Faith Cause of Action, Sections 8.01 to 8.05, inclusive. These five sections recognize that a frivolous suit should be deterred, and therefore a physician or any other defendant in a health care liability claim is given a cause of action based upon bad faith instigation of the claim. A ''bad faith'' claim is defined as a claim ''with reckless disregard as to whether or not reasonable grounds exist for asserting the claim.'' The defendant must give at least sixty days written notice of the bad faith claim to both the claimant and the attorney against whom the bad faith claim is being made. Section 8.04 limits the damages to $100,000 for both compensatory and exemplary damages. Since the State Bar of Texas had failed to certify to the Texas Supreme Court by January 31, 1979, that certain appropriate disciplinary measures had been taken against attorneys who file bad faith suits, the bad faith cause of action took effect after January 31, 1979. It should be noted that *both* the attorney and the claimant are potential defendants.

In a light favorable to countersuits, several states have enacted statutes which are designed to discourage frivolous lawsuits. In Massachusetts, Section 6F of Massachusetts Statutes, effective July 1, 1977, authorizes a court, after finding that the proceedings ''were wholly insubstantial, frivolous and not advanced in good faith,'' to award costs, expenses, and interest.

9

Lawyers in the Class Actions

9.1 ROLE OF COUNSEL IN CLASS LITIGATION

One of the many prerequisites to maintaining a class action is that the "representative party" establish that he or she "will fairly and adequately protect the interests of the class" (Rule 23 (a)(4) of Federal Rules of Civil Procedure). Named plaintiffs and their attorneys have been denied class certification where they did not adequately represent the class, because, for example, they were unable or unwilling to bear all the costs of the class litigation (Parker v. George Thompson Ford, Inc., 83 FRD 378, Ga, 1979). Class actions must be litigated vigorously and without conflicts between the interests of representatives and the interests of class members. Even the class counsel must have significant legal experience and ability to handle the complex litigation, as shown in Eisen v. Carlisle & Jacquelin (391 F2d 555, 2nd Cir, 1968). According to Cullen v. New York State Civil Service Commission (435 F Supp 558, EDNY, 1977), class counsel occupies a position of "public trust and responsibility, and in effect creates an attorney-client relationship between the absentee members and the attorney." Regulating the attorney's conduct was uppermost in Waldo v. Lakeshore Estates, Inc. (433 F Supp 783, La, 1977), where the federal court in Louisiana opined that the "heightened susceptibilities of nonparty class members to solicitation amounting to barratry as well as the increased opportunities of the parties or counsel to drum up participation in the proceedings" prompted careful scrutiny by the court of attorney misconduct.

Since class counsel's attorney's fee will normally far exceed whatever proceeds the individual class member eventually obtains, courts have bent over backwards to preclude counsel from acting both as class counsel and as class representative, as illustrated by Shields v. Valley National Bank (56 FRD 448, Ariz, 1972), where the federal district court in Arizona emphasized that counsel

> has not demonstrated competence to represent the class because he seeks to be not only the attorney for the class and be awarded a fee for his representation, he seeks in the same action, personal relief. The practice involved does not seem to the Court to comport with the high quality of objectivity, duty and integrity required of lawyers practicing in this Court or elsewhere. This case seems to involve a questionable method of soliciting legal business and such solicitation should not be encouraged.

In Zylstra v. Safeway Stores, Inc. (578 F2d 102, 5th Cir, 1978) the defendant successfully challenged the propriety of counsel's representation because one named plaintiff was the wife of his law partner and another named plaintiff was his law partner:

> An attorney whose fees will depend upon the outcome of the case and who is also a class member or closely related to a class member cannot serve the interests of the class with the same unswerving devotion as an attorney who has no interest other than representing the class members.

And in Sullivan v. Chase Investment Services of Boston, Inc. (79 FRD 246, Cal, 1978) the federal district court in California observed that the class counsel was pursuing another securities fraud case against the same defendant in another federal district court:

> The possibility that assets and insurance of the defendants who may have committed fraud against the plaintiffs will be insufficient to satisfy an alleged liability to the class of over $20 million is great enough to influence litigation strategy. The . . . interest [of plaintiffs in the parallel litigation] in collecting some money from CIS before this class litigation is concluded is obvious, and the diminution of the defendants' assets by payment to [those plaintiffs] would equally obviously affect the interests of this class.

Class actions, involving thousands and even hundreds of thousands of plaintiffs and defendants (Miller v. Fourteenth Street Associates, NYLJ, May 29, 1985, involved 585,000 plaintiffs suing hundreds of landlords for alleged mishandling of tenant security deposits), place an enormous ethical and legal burden upon counsel. Class actions today involving nonresident class members have been successfully maintained in most state courts, as illustrated by Miner v. Gillette (428 NE2d 478, Ill, 1981; cert den 103 S Ct 484, 1982) and by Shutts v. Phillips Petroleum Co. (567 P2d 1292, Kan, 1977; cert den 434 US 1068, 1978). A number of states like New York have refused to assert jurisdiction over nonresident class members unless the nonresident class members affirmatively consented to jurisdiction, as illustrated by Geelan v. Pan American World Airways, Inc. (441 NYS2d 474, 1st Dept., 1981). However, the U.S. Supreme Court in Shutts v. Phillips Petroleum Co. (supra), a class action involving 28,000 property owners seeking to recover interest on delayed royalty payments, gave its blessing to state class actions, provided that the requirements of procedural due process are met when (1) the plaintiff class members receive notice of their rights in the "best practicable" method "reasonably calculated, under all circumstances, to apprise interested parties of the pendency of the action and afford them an opportunity to present their objections"; (2) the notice must inform class members of their rights to exclude themselves or participate in the action "whether in person or through counsel"; and (3) the named plaintiff "at all times must adequately represent the interests of the absent class members."

9.2 SPECIFIC TYPES OF LAWYER MISCONDUCT

As delineated in §7.2 herein, maintenance is an offense, as is champerty, that encourages frivolous or speculative litigation designed to enrich those persons bringing the action; and in this respect the counsel in the class action situation can become an offender. In class actions the costs for which the representative or counsel is theoretically responsible are extremely high, not only the costs of notice to the class members but the costs of identifying potential class members (Oppenheimer Fund, Inc. v. Sanders, 437 US 340, 1978; see generally 71 *Kentucky Law Journal* 788, 1982–1983). Accordingly, many courts have certified class actions despite the fact that class counsel was in fact advancing significant sums of money to pay the costs, as shown in Sayre v. Abraham Lincoln Federal Savings & Loan Assn. (75 FRD 379, Pa, 1974). However, these courts have sanctioned the questioning of class counsel by the defendant or defendants as to the amount of legal costs, reimbursement, as well as queries on solicitation; in Stavrides v. Mellon National Bank & Trust Co. (60 FRD 634, Pa, 1973) the federal district court in Pennsylvania held such questions to be relevant to the subject matter involved in the pending litigation:

> We think . . . that it is proper for courts to consider the ethical conduct of plaintiffs' counsel in deciding whether to certify a class. . . . In assessing the ability of the plaintiffs' counsel to carry out his fiduciary duties to absent class members we think the court should use its "broad administrative, as well as adjudicative, power" as "guardian of the rights of the absentees" to see that the absentees are represented by counsel who is ethically as well as intellectually competent to represent them.

Solicitation is another type of lawyer misconduct that may occur in class actions, although DR 2-104 (A)(5) of the Code of Professional Responsibility does give the class counsel an "out," to wit: "[I]f success in asserting rights or defenses of his client in litigation in the nature of a class action is dependent upon the joinder of others, a lawyer may accept, but shall not seek, employment from those contacted for the purpose of obtaining their joinder." In Gulf Oil Co. v. Bernard (432 US 89) the U.S. Supreme Court affirmed a reversal by the Fifth U.S. Court of Appeals (619 F2d 459, 1980) which had reversed the federal district court; here the trial court had issued an order sought by the employer banning communication between the parties in a class action and other class members after a conciliation agreement with the Equal Employment Opportunity Commission (EEOC) had been filed; it was held that the trial court had unconstitutionally restrained protected expression under the First Amendment.

As stated in Peak v. Topeka Housing Authority (78 FRD Pa, 1977), frivolous claims may provide ample leverage for coercing unmerited settlements, and therefore attorneys filing a class action have "a professional responsibility before signing and filing that complaint to determine that there is a sufficient evidentiary basis to support the class action allegations." Rule 11 of the Federal Rules of Civil Procedure is right on point with respect to the lawyer's possible misconduct. Indeed, in Kinee v. Abraham Lincoln Federal Savings & Loan Association (365 F Supp 975, Pa, 1975) the court required plaintiff's counsel to reimburse personally the 46 out of 177 defendants who were dismissed for their costs and expenses in appearing and defending the class action. Plaintiff's counsel was simply too avid and too overreaching in the class action, and his misconduct necessitated such payments to those harmed by that misconduct.

Another illustration of an abusive class action is seen in Halperin v. Salvan, decided by the New York Appellate Division, 1st Dept., on February 27, 1986. Here the defendant attorney Salvan, about four years previous, had commenced a purported class action against the plaintiff attorney Halperin and his professional corporation among fourteen other defendants, alleging in behalf of two couples that all the defendants had entered a conspiracy "to commit fraud and usury by placing second mortgages on one-family homes under the guise of a loan guarantee and extracting additional interest under the guise of a so-called advisory fee." Apparently this class action was abandoned by attorney Salvan, and the plaintiff attorney Halperin herein now seeks damages in an action for libel and for prima facie tort in that the purported class action had been brought as a "baseless suit" solely "to inflict intentional, apparent, and foreseeable harm" upon the present plaintiff attorney. The court in sustaining the present complaint found that the privilege protecting judicial proceedings was "patently inapplicable" because that privilege pertained only to reporting by the news media:

> The present case involves alleged defamation by pleadings and affidavits. . . . [Any privilege] is lost if abused, and is limited to statements which are pertinent to the subject matter of the lawsuit, made in good faith and without malice. . . . [The statements by Salvan] were made with malice so as to injure Halperin in his profession.

Furthermore, Salvan was guilty of a prima facie tort in that he "commenced a baseless lawsuit, an otherwise lawful act, to inflict intentional, apparent and foreseeable harm without excuse or justification, solely to injure plaintiff in his profession. . . . The allegation of malicious intent is arguably substantiated by the inflammatory language describing the purported class in the caption and the Rosners' failure to move for an order certifying the class.''

''Sweetheart settlements'' are another example of attorney misconduct in the class action situation, for the attorney may settle because he is too eager to collect his fees and get reimbursement for costs, all perhaps detrimental to the better interests of class members and absent class members. But Rule 23 (e) precludes a class action being compromised ''without approval of the court, and notice of the proposed compromise shall be given to all members of the class in such manner as the court directs.'' Presumably the deterrent capacity of Rule 23 (e) requiring court approval will keep attorney misconduct at a minimum. In general, simultaneous negotiation of settlement and attorneys' fees has been frowned upon by the federal courts, as illustrated by Prandini v. National Tea Co. (557 F2d 1015, 3rd Cir, 1977) and by James v. Home Construction Co. (689 F2d 1357, 11th Cir, 1982). But the Ninth U.S. Court of Appeals in Jeff D. v. Evans (743 F2d 648, 1984) found that plaintiffs' attorneys were entitled to fees under 42 USC 1988, and ruled that the federal district court had erred when it approved the waiver of attorneys' fees solely because the attorneys' fees were part and parcel of the settlement package. This case involved 2,000 indigent children institutionalized in state facilities who sued the state of Idaho, seeking injunctive relief requiring the state of Idaho to increase educational and mental health services in compliance with federal and state laws. After 2 and a half years of litigation the defense attorneys offered as settlement virtually all the injunctive relief sought, provided that plaintiffs' attorneys waived their legal fees. The appellate court opined that ''the federal district court has a duty to review the reasonableness of all the terms of class action settlement agreements, particularly those related to attorneys' fees.'' The clear public policy set forth in 42 USC 1988 mandated an award of reasonable attorney fees in civil rights actions.

Still another aspect of the settlement or compromise situation is the utilization of burdensome discovery which has no purpose other than to obtain nuisance settlements. On the other hand, where the defendant institutes discovery of present class members far and above that required for the defense of the litigation, the net effect may be to coerce ''opt-outs'' and seriously prejudice the representative nature of the class action in the first place (Blackie v. Barrack, 524 F2d 891, 9th Cir, 1975). Absentee class members, however, are generally not subject to discovery by the defendant, as shown in Fischer v. Wolfinbarger (55 FRD 129, Ky., 1971), and abusive discovery is controllable under Rules 26 (b) and 26 (g) of the Federal Rules of Civil Procedure.

10

Sanctions against Bringing Frivolous Lawsuits and Frivolous Defenses

The merits of the lawsuit or defenses as well as the conduct of the plaintiff or appellant or his attorney are factors in determining what sanctions, if any, are to be brought against frivolous lawsuits or frivolous defenses. Unfortunately, the conduct of the party or his attorney most frequently controls, so that the more flagrant the conduct, the more dire and larger is the sanction that the court will impose. In Roadway Express, Inc. v. Piper (447 US 752, 1980) the U.S. Supreme Court established the rule that a party or his attorney who abuses the judicial process by conducting litigation in bad faith, for example, has engaged in conduct that justifies the imposition of some type of sanction. Admittedly, the court applied a subjective standard, focusing upon the personal motives of the party and his attorney rather than applying an objective standard, looking to the merit or lack of merit of the lawsuit or defense. The Ninth U.S. Court of Appeals in Malhiot v. Southern California Retail Clerks Union (735 F2d 1133, 1984), on the other hand, held that an appellant and his attorney must have acted in bad faith and also brought a meritless appeal before sanctions were to be invoked. The California Supreme Court in Flaherty v. Flaherty (646 P2d 179, 1982) applied a ''reasonably prudent attorney'' standard, asking whether a reasonably prudent attorney would have brought the appeal here in good faith. The court objectively examined the records, briefs, and arguments to provide an answer, without considering the subjective standard of the good faith or sincerity of the appellant and his attorney.

Sanctions not only act as a deterrent against frivolous lawsuits and frivolous appeals but protect other litigants whose claims and defenses are bogged down by the enormous amount of time that courts are spending on frivolous matters. (See 47 *Brooklyn Law Review* 1057, 1981.) But the use of sanctions to penalize is not without problems, for while the fear of sanctions may discourage a person with a frivolous claim from pursuing it, the person with the legitimate claim may also be discouraged in the face of possible sanctions. There are indeed several different sources of authority for imposing sanctions (see § 8.2 and § 8.3, herein); there are multiple purposes for sanctions, multiple standards for judging when an action is frivolous, and multiple instances when sanctions are imposed without notice or an opportunity to be heard, all making for difficulty on the part of bench and bar.

10.1 SECTION 115 OF THE UNIFORM PRODUCT LIABILITY ACT

The Uniform Product Liability Act, or UPLA, promulgated by the U.S. Department of Commerce on October 31, 1979, for acceptance and adoption by the several states, takes a positive step against bringing frivolous lawsuits and defenses in Section 115 thereof, which reads as follows:

(A) After final judgment has been entered under this Act, any party may, by motion, seek reimbursement for reasonable attorneys' fees and other costs that would not have been expended but for the fact that the opposing party pursued a claim or defense that was frivolous. A claim or defense is considered frivolous if the court determines that it was without any reasonable legal or factual basis.

(B) If the court decides in favor of a party seeking redress under this Section, it shall do so on the basis of clear and convincing evidence. In all motions under this Section, the court shall make written findings of fact.

(C) The motion provided for in Subsection (A) may be filed and the claim assessed against a party or a party's attorney or both, depending on which person or persons were responsible for the assertion of the frivolous claim or defense.

(D) Claims for damages under this Section shall be limited to expenses incurred by parties to the action or persons under a legal or contractual duty to bear the expenses of the action.

The thrust of section 15 is to penalize monetarily those parties and their attorneys who bring frivolous lawsuits or who assert frivolous defenses. Attorneys' fees and other costs "that would not have been expended but for the fact that the opposing party pursued a claim or defense that was frivolous" are available. However, claims for such damages are limited to "expenses incurred by the parties" or by "persons under a legal or contractual duty to bear the expenses of the action."

Aside from the question of damages being limited to actual expenses, Section 115 of UPLA has other statutory support for disciplining attorneys, to wit: Rule 11 of the Federal Rules of Civil Procedure, for example, makes an attorney subject to disciplinary action if he knowingly files a pleading or defense where no grounds support it (Barnett v. Laborers International Union, 75 FRD 544, Pa, 1977). Rule 37 (c) provides sanctions for unreasonable failure to admit averments of fact or the genuineness of documents. Rule 38 of the Federal Rules of Appellate Procedure permits a court to award "just damages and single or double costs" to a party who has been subject to a "frivolous" appeal. These federal rules are supplemented by 28 USC, 1927, which imposes costs on an attorney who "multiplies the proceedings . . . to increase costs." (See ALR3d 209, 1976.)

Section 115 of UPLA defines the frivolous lawsuit or frivolous defense in terms of what a court will determine, i.e., the lawsuit or the defense must be "without any reasonable legal or factual basis." The significance of this definition is that it allows for novel legal theories to be utilized, and hence does not penalize the innovator. But subsection (A) simply does not provide sufficient guidance to a court in determining what is and what is not frivolous. Subsection (B) further restricts the court in imposing damages "on the basis of clear and convincing evidence," as opposed to a mere preponderance of the evidence (State of West Virginia v. Chas. Pfizer & Co., 440 F2d 1079, 2nd Cir, 1971), and furthermore requires the court to set forth its findings of fact in writing. The impact of subsection (C) is that the imposition of costs by the court is on either or both the client and the attorney. Subsection (D) emphasizes that recovery is limited to expenses incurred by the claimant or defendant or persons under a legal or contractual duty to bear the expenses of the action.

Section 115 of UPLA has been adopted by several states, but each state has opted for its own version so that uniformity simply does not reign. In the state of Connecticut, for example, the court is permitted to award reasonable attorneys' fees to the prevailing party if the court determines, on the basis of a preponderance of the evidence, that the claim or defense was frivolous (Conn Gen Stat, Section 52–240a and b). Connecticut does not require the determination of frivolousness to be made on the basis of clear and convincing evidence, as under subsection (B) of Section 115 of UPLA.

Some legal scholars have placed the blame for escalating costs in litigation upon the contingency fee system, which allegedly provides a means by which an individual without adequate funds to finance a lawsuit can secure legal representation by skilled and competent trial counsel. The counsel advances all monies required to prosecute the action, such as the cost of securing and reproducing hospital records, the cost of retaining investigators, the filing and court costs, the cost of hiring experts and other professionals, etc. Under the contingency fee system the prosecution of the action is independent of the ability of the client to pay. Counsel, if he prevails, receives out of the recovery or settlement, reimbursement of all costs and disbursements advanced plus a legal fee of generally one-third of the proceeds, although the legal fee may vary from 20 percent to even 50 percent. The contingency fee system, it is argued, fosters unnecessary costs and even needless litigation; furthermore, it causes defendants and their insurance carriers to settle non-meritorious claims because of the cost of defending such cases may be greater than the amount of the settlement.

Unfortunately, Section 115 of UPLA does not relate to nor is it affected by the law relating to malicious prosecution or other intentional tort actions such as abuse of process, false arrest, or false imprisonment. It does not recognize the prima facie tort of intentional infliction of injury, damage, or loss, admittedly the more effective means for curbing the abuses relating to frivolous lawsuits and frivolous defenses.

In summary, the thrust of Section 115 of UPLA is not to eliminate the contingency fee system whereby plaintiffs are given their day in court, but to address *directly* the problem of frivolous claims. (See 49 *Cincinnati Law Review* 188 et seq., 1980.)

10.2 FEDERAL STATUTES, COURT RULES, AND INHERENT POWERS OF COURTS

The various federal statutes, court rules, and inherent powers of the federal courts all have an impact upon frivolous litigation, and a brief delineation is therefore in order so as to emphasize the variety of available sanctions at the behest of federal courts. Rule 11 of the Federal Rules of Civil Procedure (FRCP), for example, requires an attorney's signature on not only a pleading but also on any motion or other paper, thereby guaranteeing that what the attorney is asking the court to do "is well grounded in fact and is warranted by existing law or is a good faith argument for extension, modification or reversal of existing law." Rule 11 provides that the attorney may be subject to appropriate disciplinary action when a violation occurs. See Helfant v. Louisiana & Southern Life Insurance Co. (82 FRD 53, EDNY, 1979). But there appears to be no authority under Rule 11 for awarding attorneys' fees against unsuccessful litigants (United States v. Standard Oil Co., 603 F2d 100, 9th Cir, 1979), although in Nemeroff v. Abelson (620 F2d 339, 2nd Cir, 1980) such fees were awarded because of bad faith conduct. (Where good cause is shown, a party who moves under Rule 26 (c) FRCP for a protective order against oppressive discovery requests may have the court impose expenses in relation thereto.) In Eastway Construction Corp. v. City of New York, decided May 21, 1985, the Second U.S. Court of Appeals focused upon the above 1983 amendment to Rule 11. The court clearly indicated that bad faith was no longer a criterion. Here an antitrust action was brought after a bribery scandal involving the public housing rehabilitation program; the scandal resulted in the defendant city's decision not to enter into any contracts with firms that were in arrears or had defaulted on any loans. The policy was extended to prevent firms that had contracts with the city or were under city supervision from contracting with such firms. Plaintiffs controlled entities that had defaulted on city loans, and therefore plaintiffs were also precluded from contracting with companies that were engaged in city finance reconstruction projects. After the dismissal of the suit, the city argued that under Rule 11 the city was entitled to attorneys' fees. Judge Kaufman agreed with the city:

> Here, it cannot be said for certain that the firm or its counsel acted in subjective bad faith in bringing this lawsuit, or that its actual motive was to harass the city. It might just as well have been acting out of frustration or desperation. It can be said, however, that the firm's claim of an antitrust violation by noncompetitors, without any allegation of antitrust injury, was destined to fail. Moreover, a competent attorney, after reasonable inquiry, would have had to reach the same conclusion. Accordingly, the district court erred in denying the municipal defendant's motion for attorney's fees incurred in defending against the antitrust claim.

It should also be noted that Rule 11 also deters effectively attempts to disqualify opposing counsel. In Wold v. Minerals Engineering Co. (575 F Supp 166, Colo, 1983) plaintiff's motion to disqualify a law firm from representing the defendant was found not to have been based upon reasonable inquiry into relevant facts; the court ruled that the motion to disqualify was filed to harass opposing counsel, cause unnecessary delay, and increase needlessly the litigation costs. The court ordered counsel for the plaintiff to pay reasonable expenses of the defendant including attorneys' fees.

Rule 37 of FRCP allows a federal court to tax attorneys' fees to a party not cooperating with discovery procedures, and such fee-shifting is a primary deterrent to "frivolous requests for or objections to discovery." In discovery matters, as pointed out in Kropp v. Ziebarth (557 F2d 142, 8th Cir, 1977), sanctions for regulating frivolous discovery include "contempt of court . . . payment of reasonable attorneys' fees, stay [of] the action,.." and further "require admissions, allow designated evidence, strike pleadings, or enter a dismissal or a default judgment." Under Rule 37 (a) (4) attorneys' fees and expenses against parties and attorneys who force their opponents to move for orders compelling discovery are authorized. Rule 37 (b) (2) calls for similar treatment of those who fail to comply with discovery orders; Rule 37 (c), for failure to admit matters requested under Rule 36; and Rule 37 (d), against those persons who fail to attend their own depositions or fail to serve answers to interrogatories, or fail to respond to requests for inspection. Rule 37 operates when a party fails to comply with a discovery request or makes an objection to that request for discovery. In Societe Internationale Pour Participations Industrielles et Commerciales, S.A. v. Rogers (357 US 197, 1958), it was held that a person "refuses" to obey a discovery order by simply failing to comply with it; Rule 37 (a) today makes a "failure" to answer a discovery request a violation. Rule 37 (a) (4) calls for a determination as to whether or not expenses should be assessed against the person or attorney bringing the motion to compel discovery which is deemed frivolous. In Ohio v. Crofters, Inc. (75 FRD 12, Colo, 1977), the trial court awarded plaintiff almost $60,000 in expenses and attorneys' fees for the defendant's failure to produce documents that plaintiff had requested. Sanctions under Rule 37 and its subdivisions, however, cannot be imposed unless a court order has been entered (EEOC v. Carter Carburetor, 557 F2d 43, 8th Cir, 1978). The most drastic sanction, dismissal with prejudice, was given in Dependahl v. Falstaff Brewing Corp. (84 FRD 416, Mo, 1979), where defendant's affirmative defenses and counterclaims were deemed to have been made in bad faith. On dismissal of complaint as an effective sanction, see National Hockey League v. Metropolitan Hockey Club, Inc. (427 US 639, 1976): "If the sanction of dismissal is not warranted by the circumstances of this case, then the Court can envisage no set of facts whereby that sanction should ever be applied." Here, seventeen months after plaintiff was ordered to answer interrogatories, it had not done so, and the court termed such delay to constitute flagrant bad faith. Rule 37 (b) also played a role in Holcomb v. Allis-Chalmers Corp. (774 F2d 398, 10th Cir, 1985), where plaintiff sued for injuries sustained in unloading a plow by using a forklift (manufactured by one defendant) which had tipped over. Suit was filed in Wyoming, although all three defendants were incorporated in the East; expert witnesses came from other states, and it was agreed among the parties that their depositions would be taken at a given time in Texas. But the depositions were not to be taken as scheduled, and the Wyoming judge verbally ordered by telephone that the depositions be held as scheduled. Plaintiff's counsel contacted the judge's law court and tried to postpone the depositions, but without success. When plaintiff's witnesses did not appear, the defense filed for sanctions for disobedience of a valid discovery order under Rule 37 (b), and the complaint was dismissed. But the Tenth U.S. Court of Appeals reversed and ruled that the verbal order of the judge on the telephone was not valid because it did not comply with due process requisites of real notice and opportunity to be heard.

Rule 38 of FRCP permits a court to award "just damages and single or double costs" to a party who has been subject to a frivolous appeal. In Andros Compania Maritima v. Marc Rich & Co., A.G. (479 F2d 691, 2nd Cir, 1978) the owner of a tanker petitioned for an order confirming an arbitrator's award and the opposing party moved to vacate the award; the appeal therefrom was deemed "frivolous" but not so frivolous as to warrant awarding double costs under Rule 38. The court, in a footnote, simply stated, "We cannot in good conscience characterize as 'frivolous' an appeal that has provoked so extended an affirmance as the one just concluded." Rule 38 is designed to enable the federal court, in its discretion, to do justice between parties by compensating the party who has been put to the expense of defending a wholly non-meritorious appeal as well as by penalizing a party who has wasted the time and resources of the court. (See Fluoro Electrical Corp. v. Branford Associates, 489 F2d 326, 2nd Cir, 1973.) Rule 38, however, provides little guidance as to what is "frivolous"; two related federal statutes at least call for sanctions upon a showing that an appeal resulted in delay, to wit:

Where a judgment is affirmed by the Supreme Court or a court of appeals, the court in its discretion may adjudge to the prevailing party just damages for his delay, and single or double costs.'' (28 USC 1912)

Any attorney or other person admitted to conduct cases in any court of the United States or any Territory thereof who so multiplied the proceedings in any case unreasonably and vexatiously may be required by the court to satisfy personally the excess costs, expenses and attorneys' fees reasonably incurred because of such conduct. (28 USC 1927)

The decision of the Second U.S. Court of Appeals in Bank of Canton, Ltd. v. Republic National Bank (636 F2d 30, 1980), while summarily affirming the lower court decision, awarded the plaintiff the lesser of double costs and damages in the sum of $5,000 or its expenses on appeal including counsel fees: ''The appeal is so completely frivolous as to render its prosecution an abuse of the appellate process which, in addition, has put the appellee to heavy expense required to analyze the record, brief the issues and argue the case.'' Here was an action to recover damages resulting from defendant's dishonoring drafts presented upon an irrevocable letter of credit issued by the defendant bank. In the lower court, defendant interposed several defenses including nonconformity of the documents accompanying the drafts, fraud in the underlying transaction, and impossibility of performance arising out of an injunction issued in a prior case. Plaintiff's motion for summary judgment was nevertheless granted, allegedly based upon frivolous defenses, although the court wrote a lengthy opinion to substantiate this conclusion as to frivolous matter. The Second U.S. Court of Appeals, it should be noted, *sua sponte*, imposed the monetary sanctions of $5,000.

Earlier the same year the same appellate court in Miracle Mile Associates v. City of Rochester (617 F2d 18, 2nd Cir, 1980) affirmed the lower court's ruling that the action had been brought in bad faith to harass the City defendant by the plaintiffs, who were lessees and developers of a proposed regional shopping center; the complaint charged that defendants were attempting to hinder and delay construction of the new shopping center in violation of New York and federal antitrust laws, i.e., Section 340 of the New York General Busines Law, and Sections 1 and 2 of the Sherman Act (15 USC 1 and 2). The ad damnum was $49 million, and so the lower court awarded defendants their costs of defense including attorneys' fees. The Second U.S. Court of Appeals affirmed the dismissal of the complaint, apparently in full support of the lower court's finding:

Because this action is without merit, especially in the light of [the prior action], the City defendants should be reimbursed for their costs of defense including attorneys' fees. The action has been brought in bad faith to harass the City defendants. The frivolousness and bad faith are demonstrated by (1) the similarity of the present action to [the prior action], (2) the conclusiveness with which the court and the Court of Appeals disposed of [the prior action], (3) an admission of the plaintiffs in ancillary litigation made contemporaneously with the institution of this lawsuit, that conclusively refutes the allegation in the complaint that the City of Rochester has instituted "sham" environmental proceedings against plaintiffs' mall, and (4) the unnecessary and harassing inclusion, in this action, of individuals unconnected with the actions on which this action is based. An assessment of the amount of these costs should await further proof by the defendants.

But the appellate court was unhappy with the award of attorneys' fees because the appellate court was unable either "to accept the proposition that the action was brought in bad faith . . . or to characterize this appeal as one taken in bad faith":

[A]nd therefore [we] cannot justify an award of attorneys' fees to the City as costs. . . . The mere fact that an action is without merit does not amount to bad faith. . . . We therefore affirm the dismissal of the complaint but reverse the order below permitting the City defendants counsel fees. We further deny appellees' motion for double costs. As the prevailing parties, the defendants and appellees are entitled only to those costs normally allowable.

The following year in Bankers Trust Co. v. Publicker Industries, Inc. (641 F2d 1361, 2nd Cir, 1981) the same Second U.S. Court of Appeals ruled that the appeal was frivolous because "it was brought without the slightest chance of success, largely constituting an argument with the verdict of a jury which believed Bankers Trust's witnesses, supported as they were by documentary evidence, and disbelieved Publicker's." Here plaintiff-appellee had moved for sanctions under Rule 38 of the Federal Rules of Appellate Procedure. The court explored the defendant's motives:

We can only conclude that Publicker either was badly advised to appeal or was determined to delay the payment of the money owed under the judgment on the finder's fee contract to the last possible moment, in light of the differential between the legal rate of interest and the interest that may be earned at present rates in the money market or elsewhere. We wish we could call this sort of dilatory action to the attention of the Congress and the state legislature, especially at a time of overcrowded court dockets. It is an imposition ultimately upon the American taxpayer that the low legal interest rates may encourage appeals solely for the purpose of delaying the payment of money judgments.

Rule 41 of the Federal Rules of Civil Procedure under Title 28 of the U.S. Code was construed in Santiago v. Victim Services Agency (753 F2d 219, 2nd Cir, 1985) as not giving the federal district court the jurisdiction to award attorneys' fees after the plaintiff filed a notice of voluntary dismissal. On the trial level the federal district court had slapped plaintiff's attorney with a $19,000 fine for allegedly bringing a meritless suit against the defendant agency, contending that the agency was guilty of racial discrimination in firing two minority women. The appellate court ruled that the "district court is powerless to vacate a voluntary dismissal under the rule even after a motion to dismiss had been filed." In a footnote to the opinion, the court stated: "In light of our holding, we find it neither necessary nor appropriate to reach appellants' claims regarding the merits of their action against VSA or the claims of appellant's counsel that his conduct did not amount to bad faith and that he was deprived of opportunities for a hearing on the record before the court assessed fees against him."

Rule 46 (c) of FRCP requires that, before a federal appellate court can take disciplinary action against an attorney for conduct unbecoming a member of the bar or for violating any court rule, the court must give the attorney notice, an opportunity to show cause, and a hearing if requested. Rule 46 (b) provides that the attorney "shall be afforded an opportunity to show good cause. . . . Upon his response to the rule to show cause, and after hearing, if requested, . . . the court shall enter an appropriate order."

Rule 68 of the Federal Rules of Civil Procedure, the so-called offer of judgment rule, has also become part and parcel of the methods for discouraging non-meritorious suit, according to an article in 70 *American Bar Association Journal* 28 (1984), which reported that Chief Justice Warren Burger of the U.S. Supreme Court had advocated the strengthening of Rule 68

> to encourage case settlements on the merits. Offers of judgment or settlement are intended to cut down on the amount and cost of litigation. If a party refuses an offer that later turns out to match or exceed the amount finally awarded, then that party is penalized.

Rule 68 is said to exist entirely for the benefit of the defense, for when an "offer of judgment" is used and the ultimate judgment is not more favorable than the "offer of judgment," recovery of defense costs is mandatory (Santiesteban v. McGrath, 320 So2d 476, Fla, 1975). Rule 68 provides:

> At any time more than 10 days before the trial begins, a party defending against a claim may serve upon the adverse party an offer to allow judgment to be taken against him for the money or property or to the effect specified in his offer, with costs then accrued. If within 10 days after service of offer the adverse party serves written acceptance together with proof of service thereof and thereupon the clerk shall enter judgment. An offer not accepted shall be deemed withdrawn and evidence thereof is not admissible except in a proceeding to determine costs. If the judgment finally obtained by the offeree is not more favorable than the offer, the offeree must pay the costs incurred after the making of the offer. The fact that an offer is made but not accepted does not preclude a subsequent offer. When the liability of one party to another has been determined by verdict or order of judgment, but the amount or extent of the liability remains to be determined by further proceedings, the party adjudged liable may make an offer of

judgment, which shall have the same effect as the offer made before trial if it is served within a reasonable time not less than 10 days prior to the commencement of hearings to determine the amount or extent of liability.

In 1974 in Mr. Hanger, Inc. v. Cut Rate Hangers, Inc. (63 FRD 607, EDNY) two manufacturers of wire coat hangers were involved in a patent infringement suit. Defendant submitted a Rule 68 "offer of settlement" in the amount of $25 plus an agreement to cease use of the patent, but plaintiff refused the offer, and on trial defendant won on the merits. At a Rule 54 (d) FRCP cost determination hearing the trial court denied the prevailing defendant recovery of its costs, but later reversed itself and taxed the plaintiff with a $1,000 bill. In 1981 the U.S. Supreme Court in Delta Air Lines, Inc. v. August (101 S Ct 1146), a civil rights case, ruled that Rule 68 did not address itself to those cases where the plaintiff lost entirely, and that a judgment could only be "obtained by the offeree" or plaintiff. The court was obsessed with a fear of "sham offers" which it wanted to eliminate, for "sham offers" did not give the plaintiff a balanced choice with respect to potential liability for defense costs. But the objectives of Rule 68 are indeed broader, to wit: to protect an offering defendant from post-offer costs if plaintiff refuses to compromise, and to encourage settlement and the avoidance of unnecessary litigation. (See 43 *University of Pittsburgh Law Review* 765, 1982.) The highest court in denying costs to the winning defendant employer here found it unnecessary to consider whether a court might conduct a reasonableness inquiry into "offers of judgment" in Title VII civil rights actions. The dissenting opinions pointed out the anomalous aspect which allowed a defeated plaintiff to escape payment of defendant's costs while imposing these costs on a successful plaintiff whose recovery failed to exceed defendant's offer!

In June 1985 the U.S. Supreme Court rendered a decision in Marek v. Chesny (105 SCt 3012) holding that in civil rights cases (and in other cases in which courts have statutory authority to award counsel fees to a prevailing party "as part of the cost"), Rule 68 "costs" should be similarly construed to include attorneys' fees. Approximately ninety other federal statutes permit the allowance of attorneys' fees as a part of costs, and these cases comprise at least one-third of all cases tried in the federal courts (51 *Cincinnati Law Review* 889, 1984). The dissent of Justice William Brennan, however, pointed out that

> Rule 68 is not addressed to bad-faith or unreasonable litigation conduct. The courts always have had inherent authority to assess fees against parties who act "in bad faith, vexatiously, wantonly, or for oppressive reasons," Alyeska Pipeline Service Co. v. Wilderness Society, 421 US at 258–259. . . . Rule 68, on the other hand, contains no reasonableness component. . . . As interpreted by the Court, it will operate to divest a prevailing plaintiff of fees to which he otherwise might be entitled under the reasonableness standard simply because he guessed wrong. . . .

It should be noted that Rule 68 requires the offer of judgment to be made at least ten days before trial and to be accepted in writing within ten days after service; thereafter the offer of judgment is deemed withdrawn. See Greenwood v. Stevenson (88 FRD 225, RI, 1980).

In the federal court system appellate courts can base the imposition of sanctions for bringing frivolous appeals upon (1) statutes, (2) specific court rules, and (3) the inherent power of the courts. Among the many applicable federal statutes is Section 1927 of Title 28 of the U.S. Code, which reads as follows

> An attorney or other person admitted to conduct cases in any court of the United States or any territory thereof who so multiplies the proceedings in any case as to increase costs unreasonably and vexatiously may be required by the court to satisfy personally the excess costs, expenses, and attorney's fees incurred because of such conduct.

The 1980 amendment imposed attorneys' fees, and is directed to the attorney, not the client. In 1983 in McCandless v. Great Atlantic & Pacific Tea Co. (697 F2d 198, 7th Cir, 1983) the court rejected the attorney's defense that it was the client who urged the frivolous suit:

> [W]e agree with Elihu Root that "About half of the practice of a decent lawyer is telling would-be clients that they are damned fools and should stop." We refuse to accept the notion that counsel may shift responsibility for a frivolous suit to his client.

Under 28 USC 1927 courts have found attorneys liable where there was no subjectmatter jurisdiction in the complaint (Overnite Transport Co. v. Chicago Industrial Tire Co., 535 F Supp 114, Ill, 1982), or when the attorney failed to exhaust administrative remedies (McCandless v. Great Atlantic & Pacific Tea Co., supra), or where the attorney unreasonably demanded that discovery requests be in Spanish (Herrera v. Farm Products Co., 540 F Supp 433, Iowa, 1982). And where it is found that the attorney was motivated by vindictiveness, obstinacy, or bad faith, the court readily found violation of the statute (Lipsiz v. National Student Marketing Corp., 663 F2d 178, 2nd Cir, 1979). In Pfister v. Delta Airlines, Inc. (496 F Supp 932, Ga, 1980) the attorney was held to be personally liable for the costs of the defendant that resulted from the attorney's filing of myriads of motions and appeals, after waiting for four years before he initiated discovery. On the other hand, the application of Section 1927 of Title 28 of U.S. Code was denied in cases in which the vexatious conduct was the product of negligence (United States v. Ross, 535 F2d 346, 6th Cir, 1976), or in cases of parties proceeding pro se (1507 Corporation v. Henderson, 447 F2d 540, 7th Cir, 1971).

Another effective federal statute that can be utilized to curb frivolous lawsuits and frivolous defenses is the Civil Rights Attorney's Fees Awards Act of 1976, which provides that a federal court may allow the prevailing party in a civil rights action reasonable attorneys' fees. It is Title 42 of U.S. Code Section 1988, and it provides in part:

> In any action or proceeding to enforce a provision of sections 1981, 1982, 1983, 1985, and 1986 of this title, title IX of Public Law 92-318 (20 U.S.C. § 1681 et seq.), or in any civil action or proceeding, by or on behalf of the United States of America, to enforce, or charging a violation of, a provision of the United States Internal Revenue Code (26 U.S.C. § § 1 et seq.), or title VI of the Civil Rights Act of 1964 (42 U.S.C. § § 2000d et seq.), the court, in its discretion, may allow the prevailing party, other than the United States, a reasonable attorney's fee as part of the costs.

When the U.S. Supreme Court in Alyeska Pipeline Service Co. v. Wilderness Society (421 US 240, 1975) and in Runyon v. McCrary (427 US 160, 1976) had refused to award attorneys' fees to prevailing plaintiffs on the ground that such costs are not recoverable in federal litigation, Congress went to work to rectify the matter and placed the discretion to make such awards in the hands of the federal courts. The guidelines for making attorneys' fees awards are summed up by the Fifth U.S. Court of Appeals in Johnson v. Georgia Highway Express, Inc. (488 F2d 714, 5th Cir, 1974):

1. the amount of time and labor required;
2. the novelty and difficulty of the questions;
3. the skill requisite to perform the legal service properly;
4. the preclusion of other employment by the attorney due to acceptance of the case;
5. the customary fee;
6. whether the fee is fixed or contingent;
7. time limitations imposed by the client or the circumstances;
8. the amount involved and the results obtained;
9. the experience, reputation, and ability of the attorneys;
10. the "undesirability" of the case;
11. the nature and length of the professional relationship with the client; and
12. awards in other similar cases.

These twelve guidelines are operative only after the court has determined, in its discretion, that such an award or awards are to be made; there is no mandate for "reasonable attorneys' fees" to be awarded, as illustrated by Brown v. Stackler (612 F2d 1057, 7th Cir, 1980), where the appellate court agreed with the federal district court that plaintiff's request for attorneys's fees could be denied because plaintiff's attorney's work consisted of motions for extension of time, and much of the legal research had been done by volunteer law students. Indeed, the federal appellate court here utilized the denial of fees to encourage the attorney to work harder and more efficaciously, and "to discourage . . . greed.'' There can be no distinction between attorneys, whether appointed by the court, by the legal aid society, or privately hired by the plaintiff or plaintiffs, according to Oldham v. Ehrlich (617 F2d 163, 8th Cir, 1980). The court there held that the Civil Rights Attorneys' Fees Award Act ''permits no distinction between private attorneys and legal aid organizations.'' But in Alsager v. District Court of Polk County (447 F Supp 572, Iowa, 1977) a federal district court in Iowa ruled that the amount of such awarded fees should be keyed to the attorney's annual salaries and the time expended working on the case. See generally 4 *American Journal of Trial Advocacy* 371 (1980). An attorney who represents himself or herself as a plaintiff in a Section 1983 suit can collect attorney fees under Section 1988, according to the Eleventh U.S. Court of Appeals in Duncan v. Poythress, decided December 12, 1985, and according to the Ninth U.S. Court of Appeals in Ellis v. Cassidy (625 F2d 227, 1980). There appears to be nothing in the language or the legislative history of Section 1988 to indicate that lawyers who represent themselves (as either plaintiffs or defendants) should not be awarded attorney fees. Indeed, the thrust of Section 1988 is ''to increase the level of competence with which Section 1983 complaints are prosecuted.'' According to the Eleventh U.S. Court of Appeals:

> In the case of an attorney pro se litigant, this congressional purpose is fulfilled. [The lawyer in this case] utilized a lawyer to pursue her claims; therefore, she utilized the kind of skilled advocate competent to pursue legal claims, as evidenced by a license to practice law, that the framers of section 1988 envisioned. The fact that the lawyer she chose was herself is inconsequential. Thus, although we agree . . . that section 1988 was not passed solely for the benefit of lawyers, it was passed so that plaintiffs, lay or lawyer, could have legally trained representatives . . . where important constitutional rights are at stake.

The two dissenting opinions argued that a person cannot act as his or her attorney, since ''attorney'' by definition delineates an agent who acts ''for another.'' But this argument based upon semantics should not detract from the award of attorney fees because the congressional purpose behind Section 1988 ''is served by such awards.''

Another federal statute is Section 1912 of Title 28 of U.S. Code, which provides that, when a judgment is affirmed by the appellate court, the appellate court has the discretion and power to allow the prevailing party ''just damages for his delay, and single or double costs'' (U.S. v. Potamkin Cadillac Corp., 697 F2d 491, 2nd Cir, 1983; cert den 103 S Ct 3128, 1983). Frivolous appeals can therefore be minimized by the discretion of the court.

It should be observed that most trial court decisions imposing sanctions for frivolous matters are interlocutory, and therefore not appealable, and that under Section 1291 of Title 28 of U.S. Code only a final decision is appealable. Section 1292 provides that an interlocutory decision can only be appealed if an order granting or refusing an injunction is involved; but a trial court can certify an issue for immediate appeal and the appellate federal court may in its discretion permit an appeal under Section 129 (b).

The inherent authority of the court, along with statutes and court rules, allows the court to impose a sanction for taking a frivolous appeal or for abusive tactics in the conduct of a legal proceeding, as demonstrated in Roadway Express, Inc. v. Piper (supra), where the trial court had imposed attorneys' fees against attorneys who failed to comply with discovery orders in an employment discrimination suit. The trial court under 28 USC 1927 had ordered the attorneys for the plaintiffs to pay defendants' costs and attorneys' fees amounting to more than $17,000. The federal court of appeals reversed the award of attorneys' fees, holding that the aforesaid statute was limited to court costs. The U.S. Supreme Court affirmed but remanded for a determination of whether plaintiffs' attorneys had acted in bad faith; and if so, the inherent power of the court authorized payment of court costs *and* attorneys' fees. (See Link v. Wabash Railway Co., 370 US 626, 1962.) Federal courts of appeals can discipline an attorney also under Rule 46 of FRCP, but such sanctions must be preceded by fair notice and an opportunity to be heard by the court seeking to discipline the attorney.

An interesting wrinkle on the premise that courts can award reasonable attorneys' fees to curb, inter alia, frivolous matters is found in the Truth in Lending Act of 1968 (82 Stat 146), which states, inter alia, that the right to an award of attorneys' fees to the successful party belongs to the party suing and not to the party's attorney (Smith v. South Side Loan Co., 567 F2d 306, 5th Cir, 1978). An attorney for his pro se representation was held to be not entitled to attorney's fees, according to White v. Arlen Realty & Development Corp. (614 F2d, 4th Cir, 1980).

The U.S. Tax Court under 26 USC 6673 is authorized to assess damages up to $5,000 for frivolous claims and frivolous appeals by taxpayers in suits with the Internal Revenue Service (IRS). In Crain v. Commissioner of Internal Revenue (737 F2d 1417, 5th Cir, 1984) the Fifth U.S. Court of Appeals dismissed a frivolous petition by a taxpayer who questioned the very constitutionality of the federal income tax system. The court also affirmed the assessment of the penalty imposed by the Tax Court for instituting the frivolous proceeding against the federal government. The same Fifth U.S. Court of Appeals in Jones v. United States (613 F2d 1311, 5th Cir, 1980) favored the taxpayer with an award of attorneys' fees; here the plaintiff sued the Internal Revenue Service for a tax refund, and the IRS filed a countersuit for withholding taxes, for federal unemployment taxes, and for Social Security taxes in an amount seven times that which the IRS could claim in good faith. The court effectively curbed the frivolous counterclaim by the IRS. It should be noted that the word "proceeding" in 42 USC 1988 delineates a "judicial" and not an "administrative" proceeding, as noted in Prince v. U.S. (610 F2d 350, 5th Cir, 1980).

The U.S. Supreme Court determination in Christiansburg Garment Co. v.

EEOC (434 US 412, 1978) involved a Title VII action against the Equal Employment Opportunity Commission, and the court stressed the fact that "a district court may in its discretion award attorney's fees to a prevailing defendant . . . upon a finding that the plaintiff's action was frivolous, unreasonable, or without foundation, even though not brought in subjective bad faith."

The new condominium conversion federal statute (Public Law 96–399, effective October 8, 1980) is but another example of the diverse federal statutes concerned with frivolous matters. Under 15 USC 3611 (d), "a defendant may recover reasonable attorneys' fees if the court determines that the cause of action filed by the plaintiff is frivolous, malicious, or lacking in substantial merit."

In Clients' Council v. Pierce, decided by the Eighth U.S. Court of Appeals on December 5, 1985, the plaintiffs pleaded but ultimately failed to pursue a claim of equal protection of the law violation under 42 USC 1981 and 1982. But the court nevertheless awarded attorneys' fees on the ground that plaintiffs had prevailed on an identical claim made under the Fifth Amendment. The case involved a charge that the Secretary of the Department of Housing and Urban Development was practicing discrimination in public housing.

10.3 STATE STATUTES RELATING TO FRIVOLOUS MATTERS

As to state statutes, they vary considerably from state to state, and little uniformity can be found. The Commonwealth of Massachusetts, for example, under Chapter 231, Section 6F of Massachusetts General Laws, provides for the award of reasonable counsel fees and for other costs and expenses incurred in defending against claims that have been determined to be "wholly insubstantial, frivolous, and not advanced in good faith." According to Section 6F, upon motion of any party *after* there has been a finding, verdict, decision, award, order, or judgment, the court may after a hearing determine that the claim or the defense was frivolous or wholly insubstantial or not advanced in good faith. The court may then award "an amount representing his reasonable costs, expenses, and effort" in defending against such claims or defenses. Specifically, if the award is based upon a frivolous defense, the court *shall* include "interest on the unpaid portion of the monetary claim at issue . . . at 150% of the rate . . . when the claim was due . . . " *and* "an amount representing the reasonable counsel fees, costs and expenses. . . . " There is also a general provision requiring the court to award "interest" on any portion of the claim. The Massachusetts statute does not have an exception, to wit: "No finding shall be made that any claim, defense, setoff or counterclaim was wholly insubstantial, frivolous, and not advanced in good faith, solely because a novel or unusual argument or principle of law was advanced in support thereof." There is also an exception with respect to a default. The parties are also encouraged to settle the dispute so that a court award might be vacated. Also of interest are the two decisions in the annotation of Section 6F: one decision found the trial judge to have erred in awarding counsel fees in excess of statutory costs; and the other decision held that the victim of the frivolous defense was not entitled to assessment of additional interest.

Some states, such as New York, utilize protective orders to curb abuse and frivolous matters, as illustrated by Section 3101 (a) of the New York Civil Procedure Law and Rules, which provides that the court "may at any time on its own initiative or on motion of any party or witness" curb or prevent "abuse" particularly relating to the use of any "disclosure device." In Klein v. Cobb, the New York Supreme Court, New York County, imposed costs of $1,000 "in the exercise of discretion and in a further court effort to impress the plaintiffs with disapproval of their tactics"; the defendants were given leave "to enter judgment in that sum with interest from the date of default, if said costs are not paid on or before the 30th day of January, 1986." (The date of the decision was the first week of January 1986.) Justice Wright pointed out that

> [t]he present complaint is clearly barred as subsumed by the consolidated action that remains pending. Such multiple actions between the same parties for identical relief are an improper abuse of the court system. The plaintiffs are not apparently poor persons. Counsel for the defendants characterizes them as "multi-millionaires," and owners of valuable Manhattan real estate. Plaintiffs do not dispute those descriptions of their wealth. They should retain counsel. Nevertheless, they cannot be described as naifs, or Candides lost in a judicial wilderness. Their prior litigation experience, dating back to 1981 for the present line of cases alone, confirms some detailed litigation exposure and participation. Their efforts to circumvent the consolidation order and to commence new actions that, in effect, have been forbidden, constitutes a crass disregard for the spirit and the letter of earlier orders. The imposition of $300,000 costs on two different occasions and $450,000 on another, appear[s] not to have impressed them. However, such multiple applications to the court emerge as frivolous, unworthy and a costly waste of judicial time and of the time of defendants' counsel.

The defendant tenant had argued that the latest suit was barred by res judicata and that plaintiffs' pro se efforts were designed to circumvent statutory obstacles.

In McLoughlin v. Henke, the New York Supreme Court, Queens County, on February 18, 1986, took the unusual step of levying a $750 penalty against plaintiff's attorney, who had notified the court after a jury had been selected that his client was hospitalized and unavailable for trial. The court directed that $500 of the penalty should go to defendant's attorney for "inconvenience":

> Under prior practice, the result of counsel's failure to ascertain the true status of his case would only have been inconvenience to the opposing counsel. This case would have been one of several wherein juries were being selected, and any trial parts coming open would have been assigned one of the other cases. Thus sanctions would have been limited to redressing the inconvenience to opposing counsel.

Under the individual assignment system, however, the result is different. This case had been thoroughly conferenced and found not to be amenable to settlement. It had been set down for jury selection and trial in the expectation that it would occupy my part for a full week. In reliance upon counsel's representations that this case was ready for trial, no other cases had been scheduled for the next few days. A series of telephone calls revealed that no other cases on any trial calendar could be advanced from their scheduled dates on such short notice. Thus, counsel's inability to proceed left my part without a case on trial for three consecutive days.

The essence of the individual assignment system is the continuous supervision of each case by a single judge, (22 NYCRR 202.3(a)). In order to manage his docket, each judge is authorized to establish and control appropriate trial calendars (22 NYCRR 202.22). Judicial efficiency demands that, isofar as possible, each judge should manage these calendars so as to have a case on trial at all times. Only in this way can maximal use be made of judicial resources, and the entire docket proceed as expeditiously as possible.

No court can schedule cases for trial properly if counsel for the parties does not convey accurate information about the status of his case. Counsel for the plaintiff should have known that his client was unavailable, and that his case was not ready.

Wisconsin Statutes, Section 814.025, effective April 1978, represents a legislative effort to provide remedies for those persons allegedly injured by frivolous lawsuits and frivolous defenses:

(1) If an action or special proceeding commended or continued by a plaintiff or a counterclaim, defense or cross complaint commended, used or continued by a defendant is found, at any time during the proceedings or upon judgment, to be frivolous by the court, the court shall award to the successful party costs determined under § 814.04 and reasonable attorney fees.

(2) The costs and fees awarded under sub. (1) may be assessed fully against either the party bringing the action, special proceeding, cross complaint, defense or counterclaim or the attorney representing the party or may be assessed so that the party and the attorney each pay a portion of the costs and fees.

(3) In order to find an action, special proceeding, counterclaim, defense or cross complaint to be frivolous under sub. (1), the court must find one or more of the following:

> (a)The action, special proceeding, counterclaim, defense or cross complaint was commenced, used or continued in bad faith, solely for purposes of harassing or maliciously injuring another.
>
> (b) The party or the party's attorney knew, or should have known, that the action, special proceeding, counterclaim, defense or cross complaint was without any reasonable basis in law or equity and could not be supported by a good faith argument for an extension, modification or reversal of existing law.

This Wisconsin statute permits a court to assess costs and reasonable attorneys' fees, or a portion thereof, against the attorneys or the clients; unlike the tort of malicious prosecution, there is no need for proof of a favorable determination of the prior legal proceeding but only a finding by the court that the claim or the defense was frivolous.

The state of Colorado on July 1, 1984, adopted "An Act Concerning the Obligation of Colorado Courts to Assess Attorney Fees Under Certain Circumstances" (SB 182), whose preamble declared that "courts of record of this state have become increasingly burdened with litigation which is straining the judicial system and interfering with the effective administration of civil justice." The statute provided for reasonable attorney fees against "any attorney or party who has brought or defended a civil action, either in whole or in part, that the court determines lacked substantial justification" (Colo Rev Stat Section 13–17–102(2)). Claims lacking "substantial justification" are defined as those which the court deems "substantially frivolous, substantially groundless or substantially vexatious" (Colo Rev Stat Section 13–17–102(4)). The Colorado court

> shall assess attorney fees if, upon the motion of any party or the court itself, it finds that an attorney or party brought or defended an action, or any part thereof, that lacked substantial justification or that the action, or any part thereof, was interposed for delay or harassment, or if it finds that any attorney or party unnecessarily expanded the proceeding by other improper conduct, including, but not limited to, abuses of discovery procedures available under the Colorado rules of civil procedure.

However, in Section 13-17-102(7) "no attorney or party shall be assessed attorney fees as to any claim or defense which the court determines was asserted by the attorney or party in a good faith attempt to establish a new theory of law in Colorado."

While no state statute was involved in Harnett v. CBS, Inc., decided on January 23, 1986, by the New York Supreme Court, Westchester County, the court assessed the plaintiff with costs for relitigating issues barred under collateral estoppel; in dismissing the libel action the court stated that the 1985 suit dealing with a 1975 television program was nothing more than an attempt to revise "the verdict of history" and was "legally baseless." The New York court concluded:

> It does not require very much acumen to see by now that this action, legally baseless, is nothing more than an attempt to change what the plaintiff perceives to be the verdict of history regarding his conduct. A change in that verdict must result in that forum.

Attorney advertising was the subject of a U.S. Supreme Court case, Zauderer v. Office of Disciplinary Counsel (105 S CT 2265, 1985), which entailed the continuing question of how far the state bar association may go in disciplining a recalcitrant lawyer. Eight years earlier the same court in Bates v. Arizona (433 US 350, 1977) had upheld the right of lawyers to advertise in newspapers the prices and terms for routine legal services. In the Zauderer case the Ohio attorney offered in a newspaper advertisement to represent, on a contingent fee basis, any woman injured by the Dalkon Shield against A. H. Robbins Co. The advertisement cited injuries allegedly due to that product and advised the newspaper reader not to assume that it was too late to take legal action against the product manufacturer. The advertisement concluded with the statement that "if there is no recovery, no legal fees are owed by our clients." About the same time the same attorney ran an advertisement in Ohio newspapers offering to represent defendants in drunk driving cases and to refund full fees if they were convicted of drunk driving; but he withdrew this advertisement after being informed that the advertisement violated the Ohio Code of Professional Responsibility. Nevertheless, the Ohio Supreme Court publicly reprimanded him for recommending himself and accepting employment from unsolicited persons without complete disclosure as to the terms of the contingent fee arrangements. The Ohio Supreme Court's public rebuke was limited to the drunk driving advertisement, and his reprimand for the Dalkon Shield advertisement was reversed. The U.S. Supreme Court in 1985 ruled that "an attorney may not be disciplined for soliciting legal business through printed advertising containing truthful and nondeceptive information and advice regarding legal rights of potential clients." Such advertisements were deemed to be commercial speech protected by the First and Fourteenth Amendments. But states may require disclosures regarding fees and costs to prevent deceptive advertising, and the highest court upheld the reprimand for the attorney's failure to state in his Dalkon Shield advertisement that the client might be liable for costs even in unsuccessful lawsuits. States may not ban nondeceptive direct mail solicitation by attorneys to a targeted audience regarding a specific event, such as the 1981 collapse of the skywalks at the Hyatt Regency Hotel in Kansas City, according to In Re Von Wiegen (105 S Ct 2701, 1985), where the U.S. Supreme Court denied certiorari and thus upheld the decision of the New York Court of Appeals to that effect.

10.4 AWARDS OF ATTORNEYS' FEES

Sanctions for taking a frivolous appeal or initiating a frivolous lawsuit or tendering a frivolous defense can take the form of monetary sanctions such as double costs, damages, attorneys' fees, fines, and the like. The most common type of monetary sanction is the charging of double costs (Collins v. Amoco Products Co., 706 F2d 1114, 11th Cir, 1983). Double costs are delineated federally under 28 USC 1919 and under Rule 38 FRCP; under 28 USC 1927 the monetary sanction is referred to as "excess costs." The U.S. Supreme Court in Roadway Express, Inc. v. Piper (supra) construed "costs" to include clerk and marshall fees, disbursements, fees charged by the clerk for copies of papers, docket fees, and compensation for court-appointed experts, but may have expressly excluded "attorneys' fees," which are probably the most significant item. (The cost of the transcript and the cost of printing or photocopying briefs and appendices can also be significant and are included in the calculation of "costs.")

Both 28 USC 1912 and Rule 38 FRCP provide for damages as a sanction, and by a 1980 amendment to 28 USC 1927, damages include payment of "excess costs, expenses and attorneys' fees." Undoubtedly, these federal statutes therefore have since 1980 encompassed under "damages" the significant attorneys' fees. (See 1984 *Duke Law Journal* 845.) The awarding of damages rests in the discretion of the appellate court, but the measure of damages is determined as to attorneys' fees by the finding of the district court to whom remand of the case was made.

Attorneys' fees are generally not recoverable as a component of compensatory damages, unless there has been a valid contract to that effect or when a specific statute calls for an award of attorneys' fees. A punitive damage award is, however, likely to include attorneys' fees. See Dobbs, *Handbook on the Law of Remedies*, at pp. 194–204. In Ellingson v. Burlington Northern, Inc. (688 F2d 1327, 9th Cir, 1981), the Ninth U.S. Court of Appeals affirmed an award of attorneys' fees against the plaintiff based on the federal district court's finding that plaintiff had abused the judicial process and had harassed the defendants. Plaintiff's bad faith was evidenced by his filing a new suit based entirely upon sham pleadings containing false allegations that had been resolved against him (i.e., res judicata) twenty years previously before the Interstate Commerce Commission: "A frivolous lawsuit does not become meritorious when appealed." The court simply never got to the point of considering the matter on its merits, for it held that there could be no merit to the lawsuit in the very first instance! But courts do generally confine the sanction of imposing attorneys' fees to those persons who should know that the lawsuit is impermissible. In Scheriff v. Beck (425 F Supp 1254, Colo, 1974) the plaintiff admitted a plan to harass the defendant through litigation and certain outrageous conduct, and the court readily imposed upon him attorneys' fees for a bad faith civil rights action. In Curtis v. County of Los Angeles (216 Cal Rptr 635, 1985) a motorist had sued the county for injuries sustained when his motorcycle skidded on sand or gravel on a city street. The county maintained that it was a city, not a county street, but plaintiff refused to dismiss the complaint so that the county would be present at the mandatory trial conference one year later. Four months after the mandatory trial conference, the county moved for summary judgment with a request for attorneys' fees on the ground that the action was not brought in good faith. The trial court in California granted the defense motion but denied the request for attorneys' fees. The court of appeal reversed, pointing out that the legislative purpose or intent in awarding attorneys' fees was to discourage frivolous lawsuits against governmental agencies; the cost of defending frivolous suits rises when the suits are continued in bad faith.

The federal district court for the Southern District of New York in Long v. Quantex Resources, Inc., on December 12, 1985, sanctioned the award of $750 in attorneys' fees for what the court deemed to be a baseless jurisdictional motion prepared by an out-of-state law firm. Judge Owen opined:

> Under the circumstances of this case, while this Court's general rules require that local counsel be engaged by foreign counsel, Federal Rule 11 does not distinguish between foreign and local attorneys, and some attorney has to be accountable to the Court for the contents of papers filed on behalf of a client. It therefore seems to me that at the very least, a local counsel that signs the papers of foreign counsel must read the papers, and from that have a basis for a good faith belief that the papers on their face appear to be warranted by the facts asserted and the legal arguments made, and are not interposed for any improper purpose.

The very next day the same court in Hayden Co. v. Siemens Medical Systems, Inc., imposed two sanctions upon plaintiff's counsel, the first in the amount of $250 for failure to comply with Rule 46 (e) (2) of the Federal Rules of Civil Procedure, which governs objections to discovery requests, and the second in the amount of $500 for asserting an argument in connection with a motion for a protective order which the court found not warranted by existing law, or even constituted a good faith argument for extension, modification, or reversal of existing law. And six days later the same court in Harb v. United Parcel Service, Inc., imposed attorneys' fees upon plaintiff's counsel for continuing an action after his client made critical admissions at the client's deposition, "totally contradicting" the allegations of the complaint:

> It is not clear whether what is in hindsight a frivolous action was the result of Harb's misrepresentations to his attorney or whether it was the result of counsel's overzealousness. In any event, after listening to his client's deposition testimony, it was incumbent upon Harb's counsel to attempt to persuade his client to dismiss the action so as to avoid further expense to defendants.

Nine days earlier in Tenney v. Bedell the same federal district court for the Southern District of New York, in a medical malpractice action, imposed attorneys' fees of $6,625 against the plaintiffs for refusing to dismiss the action against the hospital prior to trial:

> [D]espite the complete absence of a factual basis for its purported claim against the Hospital, the Tenneys' refusal to discontinue this aspect of the action. At trial, Tenney's counsel stated in his opening that he intended to demonstrate that the Hospital was negligently responsible for Mrs. Tenney's injuries, but again no evidence was presented.

The Michigan Court of Appeals in Lockhart v. Lockhart, decided February 4, 1986, held that a court cannot order a lawyer to pay an adversary's attorney fee as a sanction for breach of ethics. The issue arose in a divorce action by a sixty-eight-year-old male who married a twenty-two-year-old female who gave birth sixteen days after the wedding; six months later he filed his divorce complaint contending that the child was not his to father. The court was adamant because the paternity claim went to trial despite "irrefutable" tests proving non-paternity. The highest Michigan court indicated that attorneys' fees may be assessed as a sanction for needless litigation but only against a party, not against that party's attorney.

On the other hand, the Second U.S. Court of Appeals during a two-year period of 1984 and 1985 had imposed double costs and/or counsel fees against clients and/or their attorneys at least thirteen times, according to the *New York Law Journal* (February 24, 1986, at p. 1). In U.S. v. Carley, decided February 13, 1986, the federal court remarked that the defendant's arguments on this "wholly repetitive appeal" are "plainly frivolous. Again he argues that income tax is unconstitutional because the Sixteenth Amendment limited the taxing power of Congress . . . the identical argument he made unsuccessfully" in his last appeal. In S & D California Fruit Exchange v. Gurino, decided February 14, 1986, the court declared:

> In view of the heaviness of this Court's docket, we can scarcely afford to countenance artificial increases of judicial burdens caused by an attorney's plain disregard of his responsibilities to the Court.

Plaintiff's attorney here had multiplied proceedings unreasonably and vexatiously, according to the court.

The U.S. Supreme Court, in Roadway Express, Inc. v. Piper (supra), where two former employees and an unsuccessful job applicant combined their talents to institute a civil rights class action against the employer, ruled that the assessment of fees against plaintiffs' counsel could not be based upon statutory authority but only upon the inherent power of the court to combat abusive litigation practices. Here the abuse tactics included willful failure of plaintiffs' attorneys to appear at hearings and depositions, failing to answer interrogatories, and failing to file briefs ordered by the court, inter alia. The highest court "authorized" the assessment of fees against attorneys for substantive and procedural bad faith.

Clients as well as their attorneys are subject to the sanction of attorneys' fees, as shown in Reed v. Sisters of Charity (447 F Supp 309 La, 1978), where fees of $2,000 were assessed against the clients in solido for filing the frivolous claim and an additional fee of $2,000 was assessed against the attorney for making an inflammatory speech one month before the litigation commenced, which speech allegedly fomented the frivolous litigation. Yet in Browning Debenture Holders' Committee v. DASA Corp. (560 F2d 1078, 2nd Cir, 1977) it was held that clients cannot be held personally liable for their attorneys' procedural abuses unless the clients were aware of or otherwise responsible for their attorneys' actions. In Acevedo v. Immigration and Naturalization Service (538 F2d 918, 2nd Cir, 1976) the court observed that the petition for rehearing was groundless and imposed attorneys' fees upon the attorney but not upon the client, because the client had a modest education which meant that the client could not have been aware of the frivolousness of her petition for a rehearing! See generally 61 *North Carolina Law Review* 628–650 (1983).

For discovery abuses, monetary sanctions have great potential utility (unlike non-monetary sanctions, which can result in the dismissal of the complaint), although they do not affect the merits of the litigation. But monetary sanctions are not likely to be disturbed by appellate courts unless there is a clear abuse of discretion on the part of the trial court. Monetary sanctions are adaptable in amount and terms of payment to any given set of circumstances. There are even statutes that provide mandatory fee reimbursement to a prevailing plaintiff, such as the Truth in Lending Act (15 USC 1640(a) (3)), the Fair Labor Standards Act (29 USC 216(b)), the Merchant Marine Act (46 USC 1227), and the Organized Crime Control Act (18 USC 1964 (c)). In the field of civil rights Congress passed the Civil Rights Attorneys' Fees Awards Act (42 USC 1988) in 1976 for statutory fee awards; but prevailing defendants in civil rights matters are not readily awarded such fees because, according to United States Steel Corp. v. U.S. (519 F2d 359, 3rd Cir, 1975), these defendants are not "cloaked in a mantle of public interest," and any fee award to prevailing defendants in the civil rights context could undermine the congressional private enforcement objective. (See 60 *Washington University Law Quarterly* 75, 1984.) In Christianburg Garment Co. v. EEOC (434 US 412, 1978) the U.S. Supreme Court declared that courts should award attorneys' fees to a prevailing defendant only "upon a finding that the plaintiff's action was frivolous, unreasonable, or without foundation, even though not brought in subjective bad faith." Two years later the Fifth U.S. Court of Appeals in Anthony v. Marion County General Hospital (617 F2d 1164, 1980) vacated a defendant fee award imposed after the federal district court had dismissed plaintiff's complaint for failure to prosecute. The court opined that fee-shifting was inappropriate because plaintiff's action was not frivolous or vexatious, at least not so without a hearing. By the same token the defendant in Copeland v. Martinez (435 F Supp 1178, DC, 1977) was awarded fees upon a finding of plaintiff's bad faith in harassing her supervisors in a Title VII dispute; and in Bowers v. Kraft Foods Corp. (606 F2d 816, 8th Cir, 1979) the Eighth U.S. Court of Appeals ruled that plaintiff had "no foundation in fact for her lawsuit and . . . this is a frivolous lawsuit maliciously filed," and the court awarded fees to her employer-defendant.

In Jordan v. U.S. Department of Justice (691 F2d 514, DC Cir, 1985) a federal district court ruled that under the Freedom of Information Act, or FOIA (5 USC 552) the plaintiff had substantially prevailed in a lawsuit against the federal government and was therefore entitled to attorneys' fees under 5 USC 552 (a) (4) (E). The court reasoned that plaintiff had met the test governing the FOIA fee allowances; but, in an exercise of its discretion, the same court refused to award fees because plaintiff's request for fees was "enormously excessive and unreasonable" and was vitiated by "shoddy documentation" as to the hours worked, as to time put in by certain attorneys in the law firm, and as to work actually done by uncompensated law students. On appeal, the District of Columbia Court of Appeals reversed and remanded, holding that the fee application and supportive documentation were not so impoverished as to warrant outright denial of any and all fees. It would suffice to provide fairly definite information as to the hours devoted to various general activities and hours spent by various attorneys; the work of the law students was deemed to be within the FOIA's statutory authorization of attorneys' fees, irrespective of the fact that the students were not authorized to practice law and were not compensated for their work.

Calculation of what constitutes a reasonable attorney's fee was performed by the Fifth U.S. Court of Appeals in Johnson v. Georgia Highway Express, Inc. (488 F2d 714, 1974), which called for consideration of such factors as time and labor expended, skill required to perform the legal services, novelty and difficulty of the applicable law, customary fee in the community, experience, reputation, and ability of the attorney, etc.

Fines are occasionally utilized by courts to counteract frivolous activity by parties and their attorneys (In Re Bithoney, 486 F2d 319, 1st Cir, 1973). Fines are paid into court under the court's inherent disciplinary powers and the money therefore does not reach the adversary to compensate for the harm done to the adversary.

10.5 TORT OF INTERFERENCE WITH ADVANTAGEOUS RELATIONSHIP

Still another aspect of the problem of frivolous lawsuits and frivolous defenses is delineated by the tort of interference with advantageous relationship. In the course of representing a client an attorney may advise or personally undertake a course of action, such as the frivolous lawsuit or the frivolous defense, that may injure a contractual, business, or advantageous relationship of the plaintiff (Newburger, Loeb & Co., Inc. v. Gross, 563 F2d 1057, 2nd Cir, 1977; cert den 434 US 1035, 1978). The liability of the attorney and his client, under such circumstances, must be balanced against the freedom of the attorney to advise his client competently and with impunity; but on the other hand, the plaintiff should not have to bear the injury, damage, or loss without some form of reimbursement or remedy.

The tort of interference with advantageous relationship consists of the following elements: a valid existing or prospective relationship or business expectancy; knowledge by the actor of that relationship or expectancy; an intentional, unprivileged, and unjustified interference with such relationship; and loss or damage resulting from the interference with that relationship (Erlandson v. Pullen, 608 P2d 1169, Ore, 1980). However, an attorney counseling his client to file a frivolous lawsuit or to respond with a frivolous defense is generally privileged to do so without fear of civil recourse, as is implicit in Section 772 of Restatement (Second) of Torts:

§ 772. Privilege to Advise
One is privileged purposely to cause another not to perform a contract, or enter into or continue a business relation, with a third person by giving honest advice made by him, except that, if the actor is under a special duty to the third person with reference to the accuracy of the advice, he is subject to liability for breach of that duty.

According to Comment a thereto:

This privilege is given to protect the public and private interests in freedom of communication and friendly intercourse. In some instances the privilege protects the public and private interests in certain professions or businesses. Thus, the lawyer, the doctor, the banker, the investment counselor, and the efficiency expert need this privilege for the performance of their tasks. But the privilege protects the amateur as well as the professional adviser. The only requirements for its existence, except when the actor is under a duty to the third person to exercise reasonable care, are (1) that advice be requested, (2) that the advice given be within the scope of the request; and (3) that the advice be honest.

. . . If these conditions are present, it is immaterial that the actor also profits by the advice or that he dislikes the third person and takes much delight in the harm caused to him by the advice.

The advice given must be honest and bona fide if the privilege afforded to interfere with advantageous relationship is to be recognized.

10.6 THE REMEDY OF LEGAL MALPRACTICE

One obvious sanction against bringing frivolous lawsuits and frivolous defenses is the remedy of legal malpractice against the attorney or attorneys responsible therefor. In Aly v. Mash (212 Cal Rptr 162, 1985) the plaintiff was represented by the defendant attorney in a dissolution of marriage action against plaintiff's husband, who was then on active military duty. The defendant attorney simply failed to assert a community property interest in the husband's vested military retirement pension. In point of fact, the defendant attorney had drafted the terms of an interlocutory decree based on a 1941 case holding that the military pension was not subject to division upon dissolution of the marriage, and had failed to undertake reasonable research into a 1974 decision by the California Supreme Court that federal preemption did not bar treating such federal military pensions as community property. The trial court dismissed the complaint, but the California Supreme Court reversed and held that genuine issues of material fact existed with respect to the attorney's negligence, causation, and damages; and that an attorney has the obligation to undertake reasonable research to ascertain relevant law, as he would be obliged to do before filing a frivolous defense.

On the other hand, in Hodges v. Carter (80 SE2d 144, NC, 1954) an attorney was held not liable for a "mere error of judgment" or for a "mistake in a point of law which has not been settled by the court of last resort . . . and on which reasonable doubt may be entertained by well-informed lawyers.'' Here the defendant lawyers handled a suit for the plaintiff against an out-of-state insurance company, and made service on the insurer by serving the North Carolina State Insurance Commissioner; the trial judge held the service to be valid. But upon appeal it was held that the service was invalid, and in the interim the statute of limitations had run against service by alternate means.

Generally persons with malpractice claims against attorneys have traditionally had greater difficulty in recovering than persons with claims against other professionals such as physicians. Part of the difficulty lies in the varying state standards to which attorneys must conform. The state of California in Lucas v. Hamm (364 P2d 685, 1961; cert den 368 US 987, 1962) deems it the duty of attorneys ''to use such skill, prudence and diligence as lawyers of ordinary skill and capacity commonly possess and exercise in the performance of tasks which they undertake.'' Theoretically, the standard is perhaps even below that of other professionals, but the courts are loathe to impose liability upon their fellow lawyers. (See 63 *Columbia Law Review* 1292, 1963.) In Texas in Bell v. Manning (613 SW2d 335, 1981) it was not an act of malpractice for an attorney for a contractor to represent to his client's customers that it was not necessary to sign a written contract. The Tennessee Court of Appeals in Taglia v. Koella (546 SW2d 810, 1979) refused to extend any theory of negligent misrepresentation to a real estate transaction in order to benefit the grantor in an action against the attorney for the grantee. An attorney's statement that no bond pending an appeal was necessary was held in Portman v. George McDonald Law Corporation (99 Cal App3d 988, 1979) to be absolutely privileged.

Attorneys have traditionally been immune to negligent malpractice actions brought by non-clients upon the basis of lack of privity (McDonald v. Stewart, 182 NW2d 437, Minn, 1970). But exceptions to this rule of immunity have developed, as the privity requisite was left to contract and was not carried over to negligence, illustrated by Heyer v. Flaig (449 P2d 161, Cal, 1969). See generally 14 *St. Mary's Law Journal* 405 (1983). Yet the majority rule, as set forth by the U.S. Supreme Court in Savings Bank v. Ward (100 US 195, 1879), holds that an attorney is not liable to parties not in privity of contract unless fraud or collusion can be shown.

There are at least two categories of non-clients who appear to be entitled to protection from the negligence or malpractice of lawyers, to wit: the intended beneficiaries of the attorney's work for his client, and those persons who justifiably relied upon the negligent misrepresentations made by the attorney. An intended beneficiary can be harmed by a will that was negligently drafted, as in Stowe v. Smith (441 S2d 81, Conn, 1981); the Connecticut court here allowed recovery by the intended beneficiary of the will against the attorney who had negligently drafted the will which reduced his inheritances. The California Supreme Court in Biakanja v. Irving (320 P2d 16, 1958) imposed liability upon a notary public who prepared a will that was declared invalid for insufficient attestation, i.e., witnesses were not present at the testator's signing of the will. The court in sanctioning liability balanced such "factors" as

> the extent to which the transaction was intended to affect the plaintiff, the foreseeability of harm to him, the degree of certainty that the plaintiff suffered injury, the closeness of the connection between the defendant's conduct and the injury suffered, the moral blame attached to the defendant's conduct, and the policy of preventing future harm.

The second category of non-clients who relied on the attorney's negligent misrepresentation is illustrated by Goodman v. Kennedy (556 P2d 737, Cal, 1976), where stockholders relied on the attorney's negligently rendered opinion as to the operation of the securities law, and were permitted to recover their losses from the attorney. The opinions of public accountants, however, cannot be relied upon by all foreseeable plaintiffs, as delineated in the landmark New York decision of Ultramares Corp. v. Touche (174 NE 441, 1931); but actual identifiable foreseeable plaintiffs, whose reliance upon the negligent misrepresentation was foreseeable, can recover, as shown in Rusch Factors Inc. v. Levin (284 F Supp 85, RI, 1968).

10.7 THE LAWYER'S PROFESSIONAL RESPONSIBILITY

Where the legal malpractice action against the attorney promoting frivolous lawsuits and/or frivolous defenses or other sanctions does not succeed, resort can be made to the lawyer's professional responsibility as set forth in the Code of Professional Responsibility of the American Bar Association, adopted by the several states. The Code was adopted by the ABA in 1969.

The rules of ethics contained in the Code are a catalogue of "don'ts," such as don't lie to a judge and don't bribe a juror, but there is also a wide area of discretion for the attorney in order to maintain a sense of professional responsibility. The Code is divided into canons, ethical considerations, and disciplinary rules, all of which merit consideration in effecting sanctions against the frivolous lawsuit and the frivolous defense. The canons are statements of axiomatic norms, expressing in general terms the standards of professional conduct expected of lawyers in their relationship with the public, with the legal system, and with the legal profession. The ethical considerations, or EC, are aspirational in character and represent the objectives toward which every member of the legal profession should strive; ethical considerations constitute a body of principles upon which the lawyer can rely for guidance in many specific situations. The disciplinary rules, or DR, are mandatory in character and state the minimum level of conduct below which no lawyer can fall without being subject to disciplinary action. Interestingly, the Code makes no attempt to prescribe either disciplinary procedures or penalties for violation of a disciplinary rule.

Under Canon 7 and EC 7–4 the attorney is expressly forewarned; "A lawyer is not justified in asserting a position in litigation that is frivolous.'' Subsection EC 7–5 delineates the role of the lawyer ''as adviser'' and states that the lawyer may ''continue in the representation of his client even though his client has elected to pursue a course of conduct contrary to the advice of the lawyer so long as he does not thereby knowingly assist the client to . . . take a frivolous legal position.'' Good faith is another prerequisite, as illustrated by subsection EC 7–22, for example, with respect to taking steps ''to test the correctness of a ruling of a tribunal.'' Under EC 7–25 ''a lawyer should not by subterfuge put before a jury matters which it cannot properly consider.''

Subsections DR 7–101 and 7–102 deal with disciplinary rules about representing a client zealously and within the bounds of the law. In the former subsection the lawyer is, ''where permissible,'' able to ''exercise his professional judgment to waive or fail to assert a right or position of his client.'' On the other hand, in the latter subsection the lawyer shall not ''file a suit, assert a position, conduct a defense, delay a trial, or take any other action on behalf of his client when he knows or when it is obvious that such action would serve merely to harass or maliciously injure another.'' DR 7–102 (2) requires a lawyer, in his representation of a client, not to

> [k]nowingly advance a claim or defense that is unwarranted under existing law, except that he may advance such claim or defense if it can be supported by good faith argument for an extension, modification, or reversal of existing law.

It would appear that the discipline of the lawyer creating problems of frivolity in commencing or defending lawsuits of a frivolous nature can readily be handled under these subsections.

Canon 9 is brief and to the point, to wit: ''A lawyer should avoid even the appearance of professional impropriety''; and Canon 6, delineating the ''competent'' lawyer, sets forth under DR 6–101 the basis for ''failing to act competently'':

> (A) A lawyer shall not:
> (1) handle a legal matter which he knows or should know that he is not competent to handle, without associating with him a lawyer who is competent to handle it.
> (2) handle a legal matter without preparation adequate in the circumstances.
> (3) neglect a legal matter entrusted to him.

DR 6–101 thus spells out an attorney's incompetency in subject matter, in inadequate preparation, and in neglect, but nowhere in the Code is there a definition of ''competence'' or ''competency,'' although EC 6–2 refers to an attorney keeping abreast of current legal literature and developments, participating in continuing legal education programming, concentrating in particular areas of the law, and utilizing other available means to attain competence or competency. In Florida Bar Association v. Abagis (318 So2d 395 Fla, 1975) the attorney apparently failed to file a suit against the original sellers of the property after the client purchasers discovered termite damage; after the clients moved out, the attorney also failed to make promised mortgage payments, make termite repairs, and make a prompt effort to sell the property. The attorney was deemed by the Florida court to be guilty of "incompetent behavior" and thus disciplined. A young Indiana attorney was disciplined under the competency standard of DR 6–101 (a) in In Re Deardorff (426 NE2d 689, Ind, 1981). He simply did not know what to do "in order to properly advance his client's matter and did not seek the guidance of any other attorney in his law firm because he was embarrassed to talk to them about his inability to adequately serve his clients."

The disciplinary rules are further illustrated by DR 2–109, which forbids a lawyer from accepting employment from a person who plans to "bring a legal action, conduct a defense, or assert a position in litigation, or otherwise have steps taken for him, merely for the purpose of harassing or maliciously injuring any person." The same DR 2–109 also prohibits employment where the client seeks to "present a claim or defense in litigation that is not warranted under existing law, unless it can be supported by good faith argument for an extension, modification, or reversal of existing law." While DR 2-109 focuses on the intent of the litigant, DR 2-102 focuses on the conduct of the lawyer. A lawyer also "shall not handle a legal matter which he knows or should know that he is not competent to handle, without associating with him a lawyer who is competent to handle,..and [shall not] handle a legal matter without preparation adequate in the circumstances" (DR 2–101 (A) (1)).

The Code has not been restricted to disciplinary actions by bar associations, for courts have increasingly applied Code provisions, particularly those relating to conflict of interest situations in legal malpractice actions, and "violations of Code are frequently treated as evidence of negligence or negligence per se" (9 *Ohio Northern University Law Review* 1, 1982). A recognition of the role which violations of the Code can play in day-to-day court deliberations means that there would be a floodgate of litigation if Code violations were deemed to be negligence per se; the burden of proof based upon clear and convincing evidence within the Code is lighter than the "preponderance of the evidence" standard in civil litigation, and so attorneys would be at the mercy of their clients and others if Code violations were permitted to serve as the basis for legal malpractice. As it is, too many cases hold that a breach of the Code states a cause of action for legal malpractice, to wit: Nolan v. Foreman (665 F2d 738, 5th Cir, 1982), Citizens State Bank v. Shapiro (575 SW2d 375, Tex, 1978), Kinnamon v. Staitman & Snyder (66 Cal App3d 893, 1977), and Ishamael v. Millington (241 Cal App2d 520, 1966).

In August 1983 the Model Rules of Professional Conduct were adopted by the American Bar Association, despite objections that the Model Rules eroded the advocacy system and interfered with the attorney's duty of loyalty to a client. Its preamble states that "a lawyer is a representative of clients, an officer of the legal system, and a public citizen having special responsibility for the quality of justice." Rule 3.1 prohibits a lawyer from bringing any claim "unless there is a basis for doing so that is not frivolous, which includes a good faith argument for an extension, modification, or reversal of existing law." Rule 3.1 further states that because "the law is not always clear and is never static," some leeway must be granted. There are significant differences between the Model Rules and the Code of Professional Responsibility, as illustrated by Rule 3.1, which prohibits any claim unless it is "not frivolous," while DR 7–102 permits all claims unless brought "merely to harass or maliciously injure another." It would appear that Rule 3.1 is a bolder step to curb frivolous claims and is more objective, for the burden of proof rests upon the attorney to show that the claim presented is not in fact frivolous. Rule 3.2 states that delay tactics are not to be tolerated, and that a lawyer must "make reasonable efforts to expedite litigation consistent with the interests of the client." On the other hand, Comment to Rule 3.1 delineates the frivolous claim in these terms:

> The filing of an action or defense or similar action taken for a client is not frivolous merely because the facts have not first been fully substantiated or because the lawyer expects to develop vital evidence only by discovery. Such action is not frivolous even though the lawyer believes that the client's position ultimately will not prevail. The action is frivolous, however, if the client desires to have the action taken primarily for the purpose of harassing or maliciously injuring a person or if the lawyer is unable either to make a good faith argument on the merits of the action taken or to support the action taken by a good faith argument for an extension, modification or reversal of existing law.

Rule 3.4 (d) prohibits a lawyer from making a frivolous discovery request at pre-trial, and Rule 4.4 states that a lawyer "shall not use means that have no substantial purpose other than to embarrass, delay or burden a third person, or use methods of obtaining evidence that violate the legal rights of such a person." Rule 8.4 (d) defines professional misconduct as conduct "prejudicial to the administration of justice," a catch-all provision that should give comfort to bench and bar seeking to impose sanctions against the bringing of frivolous lawsuits or frivolous defenses.

A lawyer's competence or competency is also delineated under the Model Rules, as in Rule 1.1: "A lawyer shall provide competent representation to a client. Competent representation requires the legal knowledge, skill, thoroughness and preparation reasonably necessary for representation." And under Rule 1.3, "a lawyer shall act with reasonable diligence and promptness in representing a client." Since an attorney must represent his client zealously also, he would probably not be held liable for the consequences of this zealous duty as an advocate to opposing counsel or to the opposing client; nevertheless, he must not commence groundless litigation . . . to avoid infliction of needless harm.''

In Melstein v. Schmid Laboratories, Inc., the New York Appellate Division, 2nd Dept., on January 24, 1986, had occasion to examine the role of the attorney, who did not consult fully with his client when the attorney discontinued the action. The court granted plaintiff's motion to relieve her of a stipulation discontinuing the action, quoting from the New York Court of Appeals decision in Hallock v. State of New York (64 NY2d 224):

> From the nature of the attorney-client relationship itself, an attorney derives authority to manage the conduct of litigation on behalf of a client, including the authority to make certain procedural or tactical decisions (see Code of Professional Responsibility, EC 7–7; Gorham v. Gale, 7 Cow 739, 744; Galliard v. Smart, 6 Cow 385, 388). But that authority is hardly unbounded. Equally rooted in the law is the principle that, without a grant of authority from the client, an attorney cannot compromise or settle a claim (see Kellogg v. Gilbert, 10 Johns 220; Jackson v. Bartlett, 8 Johns 361) and settlements negotiated by attorneys without authority from their clients have not been binding.

And in Teichner v. W & J Holsteins, Inc., the New York Supreme Court, New York County, on February 11, 1986, in a lengthy opinion by Justice Evans, scrutinized the conduct of the eminent plaintiff's counsel Aaron J. Broder, pursuant to an assignment from the New York Court of Appeals. It seems that attorney Broder was discharged by plaintiff and by her attorney for cause, attorney Broder having been hired by her attorney to serve as trial counsel at 60 percent of her attorney's fee. But a conflict of interest was present in that the infant plaintiff's father was a 50 percent owner of the defendant tortfeasor. According to the court, at trial, attorney Broder did not inform the trial court of the conflict of interest:

> From the testimony of Mr. Kreidman, who was in the courtroom at that time; from that of Mr. Malone, and the trial judge; and from Mr. Broder's own later statement the Court finds that Mr. Broder did not tell the trial judge of the supposed conflict on March 30th. The Court notes that the trial judge had no recollection of such an event. Had a judge been advised of a conflict of interest between the plaintiffs and their law firm, arising from the firm's alleged ownership of a defendant corporation, especially where punitive damages not covered by insurance were being sought, he would not have permitted an infant's case to proceed until the conflict question had been discussed with the clients and resolved. Finally, Mr. Broder's own statement to the trial court (see April 14, 1981 transcript at A 48), in which he alleged a conflict, clearly shows that while he had previously told Mr. Malone of the conflict, he had not previously told the trial court.

The next day the case was supposed to be settled for $1.2 million, but the settlement was not consummated:

Following that conference, at which the court adjourned sine die the matters of the alleged conflict and attorney fees, this court concludes that Mr. Broder decided to achieve his ends by an in terrorem motion. Mr. Broder instructed Mr. Kreidman to prepare a motion seeking the discharge of Mrs. Teichner as guardian, the discharge of Hinman as counsel of record, the appointment of a guardian for the child, and the appointment of Mr. Broder as the sole attorney with a fee of 50 percent of the settlement.

Before the motion could be made by attorney Broder, the plaintiff's father discharged Broder; but Broder still made his motion almost a month following the putative settlement. According to the court:

The evidence shows that Mr. Broder intended to use the proposed motion as a means of getting the entire fee for himself once it became clear to him that Mr. Teichner would not voluntarily agree to Mr. Broder's plan to discharge Hinman. While the evidence shows an extortionate intent by Mr. Broder, even an extortionate intent alone, not yet acted, does not itself constitute extortionate conduct.

Nevertheless, once having been advised of Mr. Broder's intention, the Teichners and Hinman were privileged to discharge Mr. Broder for cause. A client is entitled to undivided loyalty from his attorney. The receipt of knowledge that the attorney has breached that duty of undivided loyalty is itself a valid cause for discharge.

The unique relationship between an attorney and client, founded in principle upon the elements of trust and confidence on the part of the client and of undivided loyalty and devotion on the part of the attorney, remains one of the most sensitive and confidential relationships in our society. Demov, Morris, Levin & Shein v. Glantz 53 NY 2d 553, 556 (Wachtler, J.). An attorney must therefore be held to the same high standard of honesty and general conduct as any other fiduciary.

The court thereupon concluded:

Even the morals of the marketplace do not permit the use of false claims to achieve a goal. Mr. Broder knew that Mr. Woods's share of the fees had been waived. While it is possible, however improbable, that he had forgotten what he had been told in 1977, his repeated denials after reminders on cross-examination, cannot be credibly accepted. The Court can only conclude that his claim was contrived in April, 1981 and that the contrivance has been maintained until this time. This contrivance, like Mr. Broder's prior misrepresentation of the trial judge's intention, was invented as a stratagem to obtain a larger fee, an increase which could only have come about at the expense of the infant plaintiff. It was thus Mr. Broder who created a conflict of interest between himself and the Teichners, and breached the fiduciary duty he owed his clients. The evidence is clear and convincing that the discharge was for cause.

The court, in reviewing the file, concludes that the time spent, at a generous estimate, approximated 150 hours during the first phase and 200 hours during the second phase. During the third phase, in March, 1981, three lawyers devoted two weeks to trial preparation. Mr. Broder himself devoted up to 14 days to the case.

The case itself was not a difficult one to establish. It involved a claim of lack of supervision of the infant plaintiff, who had been in the temporary care of the defendants and who had been permitted to play with dangerous farm equipment. An accident ensued, which resulted in the effective loss of a lower limb. There was a great deal of medical treatment to no great avail.

Mr. Broder testified that the settlement was an unusually good one; however, his managing attorney opined that it was an amount ordinarily to be expected.

In the hands of a relatively unskilled attorney, the case would most likely have had a settlement value of approximately $850,000. Mr. Broder, as a result of his standing ability, was able to obtain a settlement of $1,200,000, i.e. an improvement of $350,000 over what might normally have been achieved.

The value of the first phase of the preliminary work is judged to be at the rate of $100 per hour. The value of the second phase of the work is judged to be $200 per hour. In the third phase the value of the work of the three lawyers, whoworked for two weeks is difficult to assess. No sufficient testimony was given as to their salaries, or, with the exception of two, as to their experience. The court concludes that at an annual salary rate of $50,000 per year per lawyer, the cost to Mr. Broder of their services was $6,000 for the two week period. Considering that the fee was contingent doubling that cost would seem to be appropriate. Mr. Broder himself gave two weeks of his time. Valued at an annual effective rate of $300,000 per year, his time would appear to be worth $11,500. Thus the total time value of the services of his firm, including an allowance for the contingency, was $58,000.

However, Mr. Broder successfully obtained an increase in the settlement by an amount of $350,000. This was a result of his abilities and experience. The court concludes that were he entitled to a quantum meruit award, he would be titled to one-third of the amount of the increase, i.e. $116,000 in addition to the time value of his firm's services. He would also be entitled to recover the amount of his disbursements, i.e. $9,403.04, for a total of $814,003.04.

Conclusion

The court has found that Mr. Broder was discharged for cause. Therefore, under an established principle of law in New York, he is not legally entitled to any fee. See 1 Speiser. Attorney's Fees Sec. 4:37; Crowley v. Wolf 281 NY 59. Mr. Broder has already received a substantial fee, indeed a larger sum than that which he would receive if he were entitled to a quantum meruit award. That fee was not computed on the basis of detailed evidence or findings. He must return the total amount to his former clients together with the interest he has earned on that amount.

Advertising by lawyers has always been sanctimoniously frowned upon by the bench and by bar associations, but in 1977 the U.S. Supreme Court in Bates v. State Bar of Arizona (97 S Ct 2691) approved for the first time the right of lawyers to advertise, although in the decision in Zauderer v. Office of

Disciplinary Counsel (105 S Ct 2265) the highest court ruled that the state of Ohio's disciplinary rules prohibiting self-recommendation, solicitation, and illustration in advertisements by lawyers violated the attorney's right to commercial speech under the First Amendment. The state cannot restrict commercial speech unless the government has a substantial interest in doing so, and can "vindicate that interest through the least restrictive available means."

About the same day in 1985 the U.S. Supreme Court In Re Snyder (105 S Ct 2874) examined a letter written by attorney Snyder to a federal district court judge's secretary after the attorney's bill of $1,900 for legal services and expenses as a court-appointed attorney for an indigent client had been returned for the second time due to insufficient documentation. The letter stated that Snyder was "appalled" by the "puny amount" of the attorney's fees and by the "extreme gymnastics" required to receive monies that did not "even cover our overhead"; the letter concluded: "You can take it or leave it. . . . You are instructed to remove my name from the list of attorneys who will accept criminal indigent work. I have simply had it." The Eighth U.S. Court of Appeals suspended him from the practice of law for six months because the letter contained "disrespectful statements" about the court's administration, and furthermore demonstrated his "contumacious conduct." Snyder petitioned the U.S. Supreme Court, claiming that his letter was protected by the First Amendment, that he was denied due process with respect to the notice of the charge, and that his letter was not disrespectful or contemptful. The unanimous court reversed, holding that his letter did not "rise to the level of 'conduct unbecoming a member of the bar' warranting suspension from practice." The court declared that "a single incident of rudeness or lack of professional courtesy—in this context—does not support a finding that a lawyer is 'not presently fit to practice law in the federal courts.' "

The Code of Judicial Conduct, also promulgated by the American Bar Association, should be consulted for infractions of conduct by judges in not recognizing the frivolous lawsuit and the frivolous defense. The role of the judiciary in effecting settlements has been particularly criticized by Professor Owen M. Fiss in a July 1984 issue of the *Yale Law Journal*:

> Settlement is the civil analogue of plea bargaining: consent is often coerced; the bargain may be struck by someone without authority; the absence of a trial and judgment renders subsequent judicial involvement troublesome; and although dockets are trimmed, justice may not have been done. Like plea bargaining, settlement is a capitulation to the conditions of mass society and should be neither encouraged nor praised.

The settlement process is in effect delineated in terms of a frivolous procedure, and such cynicism is further reflected in Professor Fiss' view that settling a lawsuit today "trivializes the remedial dimensions of lawsuits and mistakenly assumes judgment to be the end of the process." The writer concluded that when the parties settle, "society gets less than what appears, and for a price it does not know it is paying.To settle for something means to accept less than some ideal.'' Professor Fiss' theory was somewhat substantiated by the determination of Judge Goettel of the federal district court in New York in Gregory v. Garrett Corporation, decided June 1, 1984. Judge Goettel called agreements to forego certain lawsuits fraudulent, and ordered the estates of six of eight persons killed in the 1981 crash of a corporate airplane to return the $250,000 payment that each received as a release and as an agreement not to sue. The jury had found that the releases were obtained through fraudulent or material representations (*New York Law Journal*, May 10, 1984, p. 1). The decision meant that the estates are not limited by worker's compensation laws from suing the corporate employer for deaths and personal injuries.

The *New York Times* (February 24, 1986, at p. B7) reported that California's rent-a-judge, *private* judicial system, which is ''expeditious and expensive,'' celebrated its tenth anniversary, as it has become a way of life for retired judges, major law firms, and clients shunning the publicity of the public judicial system. Obviously, the private judicial system has no problems of frivolity. The State Bar of California is quoted in the newspaper article as stating that the private judicial system ''promotes the public interest'' because it frees courtrooms that ordinarily would be bogged down with ''difficult, expensive and time-consuming cases.'' Another prime reason for the success of California's rent-a-judge system is the prevalence of misconduct by California judges. In Re Yagman, decided by the Ninth U.S. Court of Appeals in Los Angeles on August 13, 1986, the rent-a-judge threw out a $250,000 sanction imposed by a chief federal district court judge against a local lawyer who had apparently been punished by the district court for alleged ''poor lawyering'' and ''history of offensive and obstreperous conduct.'' The federal appellate court cited errors by the chief federal district court judge in applying Rule 11 of FRCP which allows sanctions to be levied for improper filings of documents: ''Sanctionable behavior should be brought to the immediate attention of the offending attorney,'' but ''the fragile appearance of justice has taken a beating.''

10.8 CONTEMPT OF COURT

A court has the weapon of contempt to curb or even eliminate frivolous lawsuits and frivolous defenses, but a separate proceeding is required, either civilly or criminally, for such a drastic remedy. The power to punish contempts dates back to the early days of the English crown and the common law. Contempt of court is defined as ''conduct calculated to embarrass, hinder or obstruct a court in its administration of justice or to derogate from its authority or dignity, or bring the administration of law into disrepute'' (In Re Estate of Mekoff, 248 NE2d 104, Ill, 1969). Thus, in early England the contempt power was employed by courts as a means of punishing a presumed contempt or disrespect of the King's authority (5 *Western New England Law Review* 601, 1983). But later the contempt power represented a step in the judicial process of administering justice and securing legal rights. Today the contempt power is employed by courts to check improprieties and attempts to resist or defy the procedural and substantive integrity of the judicial process (Sacher v. U.S., 343 US 1, 1952).

A civil contempt proceeding may result in the imposition of either a penalty or a term of imprisonment terminable upon the contemner's compliance with the court's order (Parker v. U.S., 153 F2d 66, 1st Cir, 1946). Conditional imprisonment is justified under a civil proceeding because it serves to coerce the contemner into tendering performance required by the court order or decree. A civil proceeding is conducted under the ordinary procedural rules of a civil trial and the defendant receives the due process rights of a civil litigant (See 33 *University of Chicago Law Review* 120, 1965). Civil contempt generally arises from a private wrong in which one party litigant causes harm to another litigant by failing to comply with a court order. The purpose of civil contempt is therefore to compensate the injured party or to coerce the recalcitrant party into compliance with the court order. The punishment for a civil contempt is remedial and is not imposed as a deterrent. In sharp contrast is the criminal contempt proceeding, which serves to punish the defendant who has committed an affront to the court by willfully disobeying an order or decree (Gompers v. Bucks Stove & Range Co., 221 US 418, 1911). The accused criminal contemner is treated like a criminal in every sense of the judicial word, and the jail sentence cannot be "purged" by subsequent compliance with the court order or decree. Where a given act constitutes both a civil and a criminal contempt (In Re DeSaulnier, 179 NE2d 287, Mass, 1971), the court may impose on the contemner a partly remedial and a partly punitive sentence; generally the proceeding will be criminal because courts on constitutional grounds do not want to deprive a contemner of basic criminal due process rights (Penfield Co. v. SEC, 330 US 585, 1946). Interestingly, state legislatures have no authority to abrogate the inherent power of the court to deal with contempt (Walton Lunch Co. v. Kearney, 128 NE 429, Mass, 1920), nor to render that power of the court inoperative. (See Opinion of the Justices, 49 NE2d 252, Mass, 1943, and Michaelson v. U.S., 266 US 42, 1924.)

In the civil contempt proceeding the accused is not entitled to the Fifth Amendment privilege to refuse to testify (American Pastry Products Corp. v. United Products Corp., 39 F2d 181, Mass, 1930), nor to the right to a trial by jury (Shillitani v. U.S., 384 US 364, 1966), and a decision favorable to the accused is appealable (Lamb v. Kramer, 285 US 217, 1932). The burden of proof of clear and convincing disobedience to a clear and unequivocal order, command, or decree of the court rests upon the complaining person; the accused's intent is immaterial (McComb v. Jacksonville Paper Co., 336 US 187, 1949), as are his arguments of inadvertence, reliance upon advice of counsel, or similar excuse of alibi (Singer Manufacturing Co. v. Sun Vaccuum Stores, Inc., 192 F Supp 738, NJ, 1961). Issuance of the civil contempt order involves a finding that the accused did have the ability to comply with the court's command but did not do so; civil contempt will not lie where the defendant is unable to comply with a court order, perhaps to pay a sum of money (Milano v. Hingham Sportswear Co., 318 NE2d 827, Mass, 1974, and 14 *Suffolk University Law Review* 1, 1980). In the latter instance the accused must have shown in full detail the reasons for noncompliance with the court command (Hopp v. Hopp, 156 NW2d 212, Minn, 1968).

If the purpose of the civil contempt finding is to compensate the aggrieved person, the court measures the size of the penalty for civil contempt by approximating the actual loss sustained by virtue of the contemnor's disobedience of the court. If the purpose of the contempt finding is to coerce future compliance, the court considers the amount of defendant's financial resources, the consequent seriousness of the burden, the character and magnitude of the harm, and the probable effectiveness of the sanction (U.S. v. United Mine Workers, 330 US 258, 1947).

In the criminal contempt proceeding the criminal contemner is entitled to the rights of an ordinary criminal defendant, such as the Fifth Amendment right against self-incrimination.

The court order or decree that is allegedly disobeyed by the contemner must be clear and unequivocal; a patently invalid court order cannot serve as the basis for a contempt action, and the contemner cannot raise the issue of the validity of the decree or order in a contempt proceeding (Irving & Casson v. Howlett, 118 NE 901, Mass, 1981). The basic function of the contempt proceeding is to protect the dignity of the court, but a private litigant may use the contempt route to enforce obedience to a court decree or order in his or her favor, as illustrated by Coyne Industrial Laundry, Inc. v. Gould, 268 NE2d 848, Mass, 1971, where the plaintiff sought an order for attorney's fees and costs.

The contempt powers of a court are tools used to curb frivolous conduct, as illustrated by 18 USC 401, which provides:

> A court of the United States shall have power to punish by fine or imprisonment, at its discretion, such contempt of its authority, and none other, as
>
> (1) Misbehavior of any person in its presence or so near thereto as to obstruct the administration of justice;
>
> (2) Misbehavior of any of its officers in their official transactions;
>
> (3) Disobedience or resistance to its lawful writ, process, order, rule, decree, or command.

Rule 42 (a) of the Federal Rules of Criminal Procedure establishes summary contempt disposition where the conduct occurs in the presence of the court. But "mens rea" is a requisite (Sykes v. U.S., 444 F2d 928, DC Cir, 1971), and therefore the contempt weapon is infrequently utilized. A most unusual procedure to discipline lawyers was undertaken in 1985 in In the Matter of

Fred W. Phelps, Sr., by all nine active and senior judges of a federal district court in Kansas, according to the *National Law Journal* (January 20, 1986, at p. 3) against a Topeka law firm, seeking sanctions ranging from being publicly censured to being suspended or barred from the practice of law in the federal courts in Kansas. It seems that the law firm ''impugned the integrity of this court by making false and intemperate accusations'' and furthermore the law firm asserted unwarranted claims in ''demand letters . . . that sought to ''intimidate'' the judges. The Tenth U.S. Court of Appeals was asked to rule upon the matter, noting as it did prior situations involving the same law firm, the senior partner having been disbarred in 1979 in State of Kansas v. Phelps (598 P2d 180, 1979; cert den 444 US 1045, 1980). The disciplinary complaint alleged that various lawsuits and judicial complaints by members of the law firm were frivolous.

In England the Contempt of Court Act (1981) has as its objective the maintenance of the rights of citizens to a fair and unimpeded system of justice and the protection of the orderly administration of the law. It appears that the impetus to the legislation was the decision of the European Court of Human Rights, or ECHR, in the *Sunday Times* case (see 50 B.Y.I.L. 257, 1979), which involved a restriction placed upon freedom of speech by the injunction against the newspaper and which was upheld by the House of Lords in Attorney-General v. Times Newspapers, Ltd. (1974, A.C. 273); the ECHR held the English decision to be contrary to Article 10 of the European Convention on Human Rights. Sections 1 to 7 of the English act deal with the situation in which persons who comment on legal proceedings may be held strictly liable for contempt. Section 8 provides that it is a contempt of court ''to obtain, disclose or solicit any particulars of statements made, opinions expressed, arguments advanced or votes cast by members of a jury in the course of their deliberations in any legal proceedings.'' Section 9 makes it a contempt of court to use in court or bring into court for use, any instrument for recording sound, except with leave of the court, and imposes an absolute prohibition on the publication of recordings of court proceedings. Section 11 provides that

> [I]n any case where a court [having power to do so] allows a name or other matter to be withheld from the public in proceedings before the court, the court may give such directions prohibiting the publication of that name or matter in connection with the proceedings as appear to the court to be necessary for the purpose for which it was so withheld.

Section 12 of the Contempt of Court Act gives magistrate's courts in England the power to deal with any person who willfully insults any justice, witness, court official, or lawyer having business in the court, either in the courtroom or in going to or returning from proceedings of the court, or who otherwise misbehaves in court. Such a person may be detained until the rising of that court and may be imprisoned for up to thirty days, fined up to £ 500, or both.

Section 13 enables legal aid to be granted in respect of proceedings for contempt. See generally 45 *Modern Law Review* (England) 301 (May 1982).

10.9 SECURITY FUNDS FOR AGGRIEVED PERSONS

After the horse has been stolen, the barn door must be locked, and a Clients' Security Fund, like the New York statute, is one example of legislative efforts to right the wrong that could have resulted from "dishonest conduct" of an attorney, in perhaps pushing forth a frivolous lawsuit or a frivolous defense. The New York statute defines its purpose as the promotion of "public confidence in the administration of justice and the integrity of the legal profession by reimbursing losses caused by the dishonest conduct of attorneys admitted and licensed to practice law in the courts of New York State." Under Section 7200.8 "eligible claims" are delineated as losses caused by dishonest acts of attorneys, provided that "(a) the dishonest conduct alleged in the claim constituted the misappropriation or willful misapplication of a client's money, security, or other property." Subparagraph (c) requires that the claim be made "directly by the client or the client's representative," thereby restricting the claim to clients of that attorney, not opposing parties who may be harmed by the dishonest conduct of the attorney. According to the *New York Law Journal* (January 13, 1986, p. 1), the fund in 1985 paid out twenty-six awards totaling $220,669, or an aggregate total of $2.8 million to 807 persons since the fund began operating in December 1982.

The New York State Clients' Security Fund figured in a federal district court case, Tedesco v. Mishkin, decided on February 28, 1986. It appears that a class action was brought against defendant attorney, his company, the Bank of New York, and his former law partners and employees by some 300 persons who alleged that defendants had conducted an illegal scheme to obtain investment funds amounting to $12 million. Plaintiffs' lawyers were authorized by the federal district court for the Southern District of New York to write in December 1983 to the class, informing them that if they had dealings with Mishkin or his former law firm, they might be able to claim partial reimbursement from the New York State Clients' Security Fund. One of the plaintiffs, Winer, for whom Mishkin was a lawyer and investment confidant for almost thirty years, was angered by the letter, and so he allegedly drafted a letter (later determined by the court to be written by Mishkin); this Winer-Mishkin letter stated that plaintiffs' lawyers were waging a "vicious campaign" to discredit Mishkin and that plaintiffs' lawyers would charge substantial legal fees. The letter also stated that Winer did not want to be represented by these lawyers and urged other class members to seek other counsel. The court decided that this Winer-Mishkin letter was "materially false and misleading . . . and was known by Mishkin to be false and misleading at the time he prepared the letter." Mishkin, according to the court, had aided and abetted Winer to commit perjury in Winer initially claiming that he alone wrote the letter; Mishkin also testified falsely in court that he had not written the letter. The court thereupon imposed sanctions exceeding $75,000 against attorney Mishkin, which amount included $10,000 as punitive damages. Mishkin was also ordered at his own expense by the court to send another explanatory letter, together with a copy of the court's thirty-one page opinion, to the entire class. The monetary sanctions were the counsel fees and costs spent by other lawyers in uncovering proof of Mishkin's "misconduct."

A similar fund operates in the criminal field to aid victims of crime. Article 22 of the New York Executive Law is one example of a vehicle to provide aid, care, and support to victims of crimes in the state of New York. Crime victims in New York are even given the opportunity to participate in the proceedings and parole hearings and have a right to be informed of the discharge, parole, or escape of the criminal who caused their disability.

10.10 PUNITIVE DAMAGE AWARDS

It would appear that the majority of jurisdictions sanctioning awards for punitive damages justify such awards on the basis of punishment and deterrence. Indeed, the punitive damage award is a type of "private tax" assessed against the particular tortfeasor for conduct that is repulsive, to say the least. See 56 *Southern California Law Review* 155 (1982). It is therefore understandable why insurance for punitive damages is generally against public policy, as illustrated by Northwestern National Co. v. McNulty (307 F2d 432, 5th Cir, 1962): "The damages [should] rest ultimately . . . on the party actually responsible for the wrong."

The popularity of punitive damage awards is readily evident from the volume of such awards as well as the huge amounts of such awards. Yet there are baseless and extravagant punitive damage claims assserted without foundation in law or in fact, and the courts are therefore required to take action to curb such frivolity. In Slapikas v. Credit Lyonnais, the federal district court for the Southern District of New York, on December 11, 1985, granted a motion for summary judgment dismissing a cause of action for punitive damages in a wrongful discharge case, holding that the claim was "frivolous":

> It is well established that there is no independent action for punitive damages in New York [citations omitted]. Additionally, punitive damages are not permitted in a breach of contract action in New York absent "fraud aimed at the public generally, evincing a high degree of moral turpitude and demonstrating such wanton dishonesty as to imply a criminal indifference to civil obligations."

The court found that the plaintiff's pleading contained "no facts that suggest the kind of morally reprehensible behavior calling for exemplary damages."

Six days earlier the same court in International Television Productions, Ltd.

v. Twentieth Century Fox Television had dismissed baseless punitive damage claims:

> Viewed in the light most favorable to the plaintiffs . . . [the pleadings] contains allegations of run-of-the-mill fraud involving the intentional misstatement of financial projections and financial reports. The amended complaint does not allege gross or wanton conduct or criminal indifference to civil obligations. An award of punitive damages is inappropriate in these circumstances.

10.11 AMERICAN BAR ASSOCIATION RECOMMENDATIONS AND SUGGESTIONS

In 1984 the American Bar Association published a comprehensive report entitled "Towards a Jurisprudence of Injury: The Continuing Creation of a System of Substantive Justice in American Tort Law." The ABA report, embracing fourteen chapters, explored the tort system in great detail, a system that "has become a mirror of American society, held up to some of its most difficult moments of private conflict." Chapter 13 sets forth the "recommendations and suggestions" which are derived from the tort system's "incremental, case-centered approach, and from its status as a decentralized and constantly experimental feature of a federal system."

Of the ten recommendations and suggestions, "Judicial Case Management," requiring that "every court handling civil cases should establish protocols designed to increase judicial efficacy," appears to attack the problem of "the unfortunate tendency of some attorneys to introduce complicating factors into litigation unrelated either to the merits or to the appropriate use of existing procedural rules." Favorably considered here is the 1983 amendment to Rule 11 of the Federal Rules of Civil Procedure that requires attorneys to certify motions and other papers as being in good faith; a simultaneous amendment to Rule 26 also imposed a requirement of good faith to control "both excessive discovery and evasion" by "explicitly encouraging the imposition of sanctions." Lawyers are encouraged to respect "their professional responsibility to avoid dilatory and obfuscatory tactics." The ABA report emphasized that "professional organizations should interest themselves more seriously in disciplining lawyers who tie up judicial resources with litigation without arguable merit." However, "the characterization of some litigation as frivolous must avoid the trap of making the law a bastion of privilege":

> The problem lies in the fact that not infrequently, suits criticized as frivolous today may generate tomorrow's law. The balance is a delicate one. Yet we acknowledge that a certain percentage of suits which occupy the time of American courts are of legal value so doubtful that lawyers ought not to have brought them.

The *National Law Journal* (February 3, 1986, at p. 3) reported that a business-oriented American Tort Reform Association (ATRA), representing more than 900,000 Americans, had publicly proclaimed: "Our country can no longer afford a deep-pocket tort system." Among the reforms advocated by this new organization are alteration of the contingency fee system so as to reduce the percentage of awards taken by lawyers, restrictions on the use of joint and several liability, and limitation of awards for non-economic losses such as pain and suffering. ATRA is also working for the adoption by states of model bills for overall tort reform.

Bibliography

Baird, Peter D. ''Ballooning Toward a New Due Diligence for Litigators.'' 20 Ariz B J 22–26 (Feb.-Mar. 1985).

Burbank, Stephen B. ''Sanctions in the Proposed Amendments to the Federal Rules of Civil Procedure: Some Questions About Power (The Role of the Judge in Tort Law).'' 11 Hofstra L Rev 997–1011 (Spring 1983).

Cann, Wesley A. ''Frivolous Lawsuits-The Lawyer's Duty to Say 'No'.'' 31 Def L J 24–51 (Jan.-Feb. 1982).

Davis, Glenn E. ''Prevailing Defendant Fee Awards in Civil Rights Litigation: A Growing Threat to Private Enforcement.'' 60 Wash U L Q 75–118 (Spring 1982).

Epstein, Edna S.; Corcoran, C Timothy III; Krieger, Frederick M.; and Carr, William B. ''An Up-date on Rule 37 Sanctions after National Hockey League v. Metropolitan Hockey Clubs, Inc.'' 84 FRD 145–173 (Jan. 1980).

Forucci, Glenn D.; Roland, Richard R.; and Stalcup, Nancy K. ''Frivolous Appeals (Calif Sup Ct Survey, Jan. to June 1982).'' 10 Pepperdine L Rev 174–177 (Dec. 1982).

Goodman, Richard S. ''The Frivolous Case or Everybody Makes Money but the Doctor.'' 10 Leg Asp Med Pract 7–88 (Mar. 1982).

Hurley, Dan. ''Much Ado About Nothing: An Epidemic of Frivolous Law Suits Is Turning Our Legal System into the Courtroom of the Absurd.'' 17 Docket Call 14–17 (Summer 1982).

Kasdan, David S. ''A Uniform Approach to New York State Liability for Wrongful Imprisonment: A Statutory Mode.'' 49 Alb L Rev 201–243 (Fall 1984).

Larsen, Jeffrey R. ''Massachusetts Prohibits Withdrawal by Court-Appointed Counsel from Potentially Frivolous Appeals.'' 16 Suffolk U L Rev 280–295 (Spring 1982).

Loth, Ellen. ''Appealing the Frivolous Appeal.'' 56 Ohio St B A Rep 1630(6) (Nov. 14, 1983).

McKirdy, Charles R. "28 USC 1927-Counselor Beware." 71 Ill N J 708–712 (Aug. 1983).

Martineau, Robert J. "Frivolous Appeals: The Uncertain Federal Response." 1984 Duke L J 845–886 (Nov. 1984).

Meadows, Alice T. "A Frivolous Lawsuit May Destroy the Career of a Professional: Is There No Remedy?" 17 U Rich L Rev 421–437 (Winter 1983).

Newman, Thomas R. "Frivolous Appeals." 188 NYLJ (Dec. 16, 1982), p. 1, col. 1.

Oberman, Michael S. "Federal Courts: Commentary: Coping with Rising Caseload: Defining the Frivolous Civil Appeal." 42 Brooklyn L Rev 1057–1074 (Spring 1981).

Olson, Ronald L., and McConnell, Stephen J. "Deterring and Defeating Frivolous and Abusive Litigation." 27 For Defense 16–25 (Jan. 1985).

Owen, David G. "Countersuits Against Attorneys-A Preface." 33 SC L Rev 313–315 (Dec. 1981).

Parness, Jeffrey. "Groundless Pleadings and Certifying Attorneys in the Federal Courts." 1985 Utah L Rev 325–371 (Spring 1985).

Rawson, Jean. "Wong v. Taylor: The Latest Word in Physician-Attorney Countersuits." 17 Val U L Rev 755–765 (Summer 1983).

Reskin, Lauren R. "Rule 11 Requires More Than Subjective Good Faith." 71 ABAJ 132 (2) (Oct. 1985).

Russell, Ronald G. "Denial of Millions in Costs and Attorney's Fees as a Discovery Sanction." 1982 Utah L Rev 445–459 (Spring 1982).

Salter, William E. "Abuse of Process." 33 SC L Rev 331–342 (Dec. 1981).

Schwartz, Victor E. "The Uniform Product Liability Act: A Brief Overview." 33 Vand L Rev 579–592 (Apr. 1980).

Shaneyfelt, David A. "Courts Are No Place for Fun and Frivolity: A Warning to Vexatious Litigants and Over-zealous Attorneys." 20 Williamette L Rev 441–493 (Summer 1984).

Sherwood, Richard W. "Curbing Discovery Abuse: Sanctions under the Federal Rules of Civil Procedure and the California Code of Civil Procedure." 21 Santa Clara L Rev 567–611 (Summer 1981).

Snyder, Jean M. "The Chill of Rule 11." 11 Litig 16(4) (Winter 1985).

Stanfield, Sandra V. "Combatting Vexatious Family Law Litigation by Imposing Attorney's Fees as Sanctions." 12 San Fern V L Rev 59–76 (Spring 1984).

Stephenson, Gail W. "Damages for Frivolous Appeal." 45 La L Rev 137–148 (Sept. 1984).

Stonehill, David N. "Aligning Policy with Theory: The Uniform Product Liability Act's Apportionment of Responsibility in Product Liability Actions." 49 U Cinn L Rev 162–186 (Winter 1980).

Index to Cases

Subject Index

About the Author

WARREN FREEDMAN, a member of the New York, Federal, and U.S. Supreme Court bars, served as corporate counsel to Bristol-Myers Company for 20 years in addition to his private law practice. He is the author of *International Products Liability* (3 vols.), *Products Liability for Corporate Counsels, Controllers, and Product Safety Executives, Allergy and Products Liability, Richards on Insurance,* and *The Right of Privacy in the Computer Age* (Greenwood Press, 1987) as well as two travel books and three sociology textbooks. Over the years he has contributed extensively to various law journals and reviews. He has taught on the graduate level at Rutgers University School of Law and the New School for Social Research.